W9-COA-784

F Quilt and Sew FANCIFUL FOLK ART

MIRIAM GOURLEY

©2004 Miriam Gourley

Published by

kp books
An imprint of F+W Publications, Inc.

700 East State Street • Iola, WI 54990-0001
715-445-2214 • 888-457-2873

Our toll-free number to place an order or obtain a free catalog is 800-258-0929.

All rights reserved. No portion of this publication may be reproduced or transmitted in any form or by any means, electronic or mechanical, including photocopy, recording, or any information storage and retrieval system, without permission in writing from the publisher, except by a reviewer who may quote brief passages in a critical article or review to be printed in a magazine or newspaper, or electronically transmitted on radio, television or the Internet.

Library of Congress Catalog Number: 2004093857
ISBN: 0-87349-843-7
Edited by Nicole Gould and Candy Wiza
Designed by Donna Mummery and Marilyn McGrane

Printed in the United States of America

Acknowledgments

This book is for Sonia—my sister, my friend and earliest sewing buddy. She always patiently unpicked her mistakes. I threw mine away. May she sometime have time to pick up a needle and thread and make quilts for the two "boys" in her life.

Also, many thanks to my friends at Bernina®, EK Success LTD.©, Fabric Country, Dan River Inc.©, Fairfield Processing Inc. and Michael Miller Fabrics©. You all are terrific!

Table of Contents

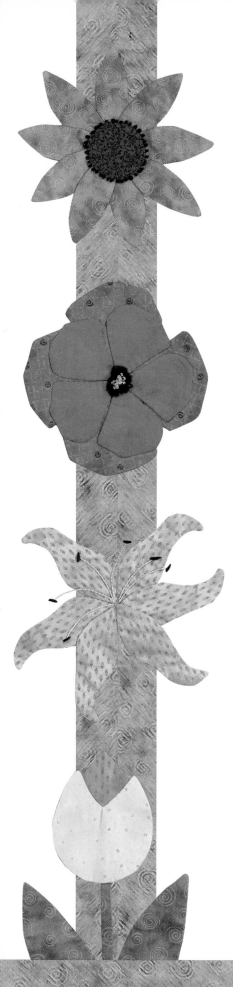

Summer

Autumn

Winter

Introduction

If you are looking for a quilt with precise, mathematical piecework, run away now. I never felt inspired by mathematics. If you are, however, looking for a book that explores texture, color, wonderful whimsy and personality, you might want to settle yourself into a comfortable chair and get ready for a new adventure.

I simply cannot write a book without telling stories. Every doll and quilt I make has ingredients that go beyond the normal fabric, pins and needles. I suppose we all dwell on happy moments in our past and hopeful dreams for our futures. Somewhere in all this madness, we all yearn for a simpler time, with visits with neighbors across the fence, the casual dinner in the backyard with cherished family and friends, and time to contemplate. Stitching "forces" us to take things a little slower, gives us time to think, and yields the satisfaction of a tangible result of time spent.

The projects in this book are arranged in seasonal categories, although most of the projects are appropriate for year-round decor. I enjoy the changing seasons. When each new season approaches, I find myself cleaning my house like mad. The car is filled with discarded treasures to go to Goodwill and become someone else's treasures, and I clean windows, curtains, cupboards, and dust everything thoroughly. Then, up goes the appropriate seasonal decorations, and the house feels fresh and ready to fill with favorite people. Quilts are an important aspect of the seasonal changes, whether it's removing the extra quilt from the bed as spring comes, or hanging a special holiday quilt as fall approaches.

Adding unexpected embellishments, like scrapbook hardware, hand-inked captions on fabric, hand-painted wooden buttons, in fact, any kind of button is a bit of a trademark for me. I like to create things that people want to reach out and touch—and, of course, I let them do that. I also like practical quilts—those that are big enough to spread across your bed, if the winter is a little chilly, or to wrap around yourself when you see a scary movie! Quilts originally were created for comfort, and I like mine to do that, too. Sometimes, quilts can give you visual comfort, too. The Old Crow Farm quilt does that for me.

This book is meant to inspire you to make quilts. This book also is meant to inspire you to create your own versions or to use some of the techniques to branch out in a totally different avenue. Build your dreams into the projects you make. Celebrate the good things in your life with your quilt making and sewing. We all spend far too much time on the treadmill. My good friend, Jane, passed along some sage advice from her father: "Make sure you take a vacation each day." That might be reading your favorite book just before you drop off to sleep, or taking a few minutes to add some stitches to your newest quilt. I hope this book will afford a little vacation for those who peruse the pages. Happy quilting!

Miriam Gourley

Basic Quilting Techniques

Miriam's Favorite Appliqué Method

This whole method is not new; I refer to it as Double Appliqué. I find it to be the easiest way to achieve nice rounded edges without burning your fingers with an iron, working with butcher paper, needle turning, or using any of the other more traditional methods. I love the look of appliqué for the extra dimension it adds to quilting.

STEP 1 * Place your pattern on a piece of doubled fabric. Doubled fabric is two pieces of fabric positioned with right sides together. Use a pencil to trace around the pattern shape, right on the fabric. The pencil line will be your stitching line. Stitch on the pencil line, sewing both layers of fabric together.

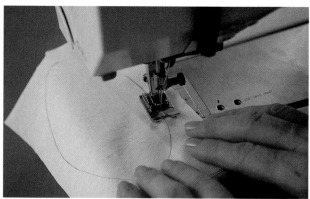

STEP 2 * If your fabric is too dark or busy to see the pencil line, you can pin the pattern piece right to the fabric and stitch around the paper edge.

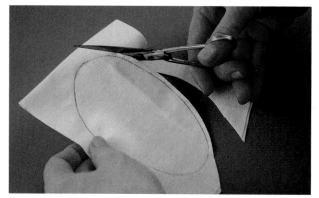

STEP 3 * Cut out the appliqué ¼" or less from the sewn line. Trim the seam allowance.

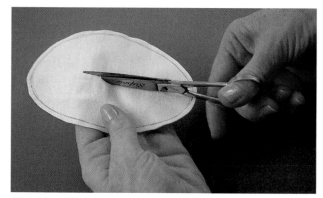

STEP 4 * Without turning the fabric over, make a slit through the top layer of fabric. Make sure you only cut through one layer! The slit needs to be just large enough to turn the fabric right side out.

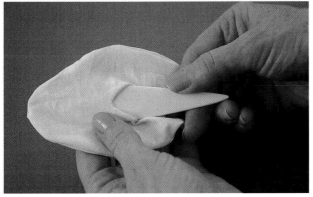

STEP 5 * Turn the fabric right side out, and use a tool to gently round out the edges, and push out the corners.

STEP 6 * Press the fabric on your ironing board.

STEP 7 * Some pieces are layered together, and may use felt on top of the fabric, or felt below, to outline the piece. Layer and stitch these pieces together before you attach them to the quilt. You will use a straight stitch for most designs, but sometimes I have made the stitches less visible, such as the clothing on Queen of the Harvest above.

Transferring Embroidery Designs

Most of the time, you can just place your fabric on the pattern over a light table, a television screen or your window to trace the design with a No. 2 lead pencil. When the fabric is too dark, you can use a white tracing pencil, available at sewing supply stores.

If the fabric is too thick or the texture is wrong there are alternatives:

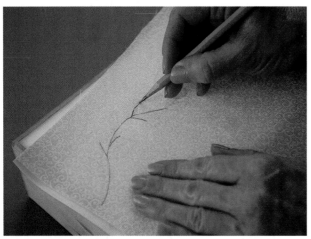

STEP 1 * Photocopy the pattern, and use an iron-transfer pen or pencil to outline the figure on the wrong side of the paper. You can see it easily on a light table, window or computer screen.

STEP 2 * This method also is useful to transfer a face to a finished Double Appliqué shape, as it is difficult to use a tracing method.

STEP 3 * Follow the directions on the package to heat up your iron to the proper temperature. Usually, you need to turn the steam off and use a dry iron. Iron the design onto the fabric, pencil side toward fabric, keeping the heat on the pattern only long enough for you to really see the design clearly. If you leave the iron on too long, you will have thick lines, which will be difficult to cover with embroidery work.

STEP 4 * Remove the paper and proceed with the embroidery.

Tubing and Celtic Work

Most of the time, appliqué pieces with parallel edges, such as legs or plant stems, can be stitched as a tube and then turned right-side out. When the tubes are too small, or the tubes need to be curved, you can easily achieve that look with a little know-how.

STEP 1 * Cut a piece of fabric on a 45-degree angle (bias cut). Turn the fabric, so the bias side is at the top, and trim off any crooked edge.

STEP 2 * Use your rotary cutter to cut bias strips (any width you choose).

STEP 3 * Use your iron to press the strips in half, wrong sides together.

STEP 4 * Pencil the line you want to follow on the quilt top, and pin the raw edges of the bias along the line.

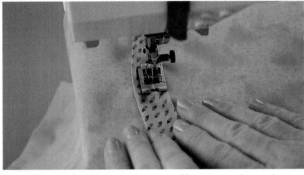

STEP 5 * Machine stitch, just off-center, along the bias strip. Make sure you can fold the folded edge over and cover the raw edges after stitching.

STEP 6 * Fold the folded edge over to cover the raw edges, and press.

STEP 7 * Hand stitch in place.

Assembling the Quilt

When all the embellishments have been stitched in place and the quilt top is pleasing to you, it is time to finish the quilt. As you go through the steps below, you will see your quilt gain dimension and texture through the addition of layers of batting, backing and quilting. Once the quilt is bound, which to me is like adding a frame to a picture, your quilt is ready. It's like preparing a sumptuous meal—now it's time to feast!

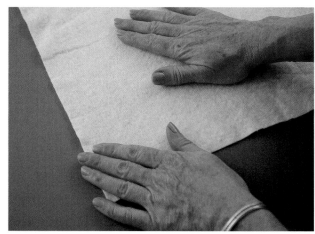

STEP 1 * Assemble the backing. If it needs to be pieced together, be sure to press the seams open. Make sure the backing is pressed well before you start. I recommend that you leave the backing about 4" larger than the quilt top on each side.

STEP 2 * Place the batting on a large worktable or on the floor, and cut the batting to fit the backing (including the extra 4", see Step 1).

STEP 3 * Spread the batting on the table or floor, and smooth it so there are no wrinkles.

STEP 4 * Spray the back of your quilt top with basting spray. Basting spray is a wonderful invention, and I heartily recommend it to any of you who have had your quilts shift while quilting. You must spray it out-of-doors or in a protected area. You don't want the mist to settle on your carpet or floor and become a dirt magnet. If the quilt is large, I suggest you have a partner help you.

STEP 5 * After the spray is applied, carefully smooth the top onto the batting. You can lift and re-position the top, if you need to. Use your hands, and start in the middle, working outward.

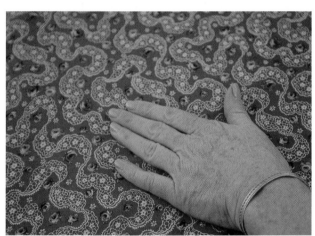

STEP 6 * Turn the quilt over so the batting is face up. Spray the backing, and smooth it onto the batting.

STEP 7 * Use a few safety pins to baste larger quilts, as a safety precaution. Machine stitch about ¼" from the edge of the quilt top, and trim off the excess fabric and batting. The quilt is ready for whatever method you choose to quilt it.

Note: *The basting spray will wash out (if you can wash the quilt), but also over time, just disintegrates, without harming the fabric at all.*

Binding

Binding a quilt with mitered corners used to terrify me, but it has become as easy as pie. I taught my then-17-year-old daughter, Vanessa, and she is very proficient at it.

There are two very similar methods of binding. One involves a double layer of fabric, which is good for quilts that really get used for snuggling and for bedding. The double layer prevents the binding from wearing out so fast. The single layer of binding is stitched to the quilt in the same way, but is better for wall quilts and table runners, as the binding isn't quite as bulky.

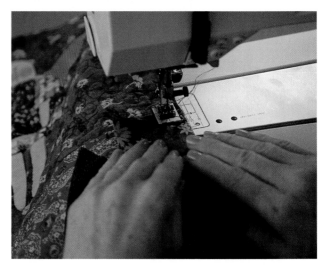

STEP 1 ✳ Most of the binding in this book is either 2½" wide or 5". (The 5" is pressed in half, wrong sides together.) Cut the indicated number of strips, and sew them end to end, with the seams pressed open.

STEP 2 ✳ Press under ¼" of one end of the strip, and place it on the edge of the quilt top (never begin at a corner), with the raw edges together.

STEP 3 ✳ Stitch the binding to the quilt, stitching a scant ⅝" from the raw edges. Stop the stitching ⅝" from the corner.

STEP 4 ✳ Fold the binding upward at a 90-degree angle from the top quilt edge.

STEP 5 * Fold the binding back down again, with the raw edges of the quilt and binding even.

STEP 6 * Begin stitching ⅝" from the corner, and repeat this sequence at each corner.

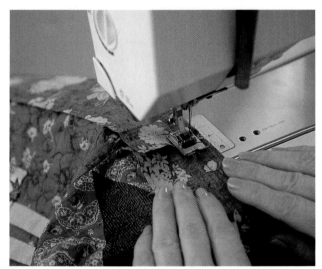

STEP 7 * Overlap the binding ⅜", and cut off the excess binding.

STEP 8 * If the binding is the 5" width, bring the folded edge over to the back side to cover the machine stitching. Hand stitch to the back of the quilt.

STEP 9 * If the binding is the 2½" width, you will need to fold under approximately ½" of the raw edge to cover the previous stitching. Hand stitch the folded edge to the back of the quilt.

STEP 10 * Fold under the raw edge, and stitch to the back of the quilt. Be sure to miter the corners so they look the same as the front side. Stitch by hand.

Attaching Cording

Sometimes a corded edge is a great accent for the edge of a quilt or pillow. Some of the large cording is a little overwhelming to use if you don't know some of the tricks.

STEP 1 * Unravel about 1" of the end of the cording, so it can lie flat.

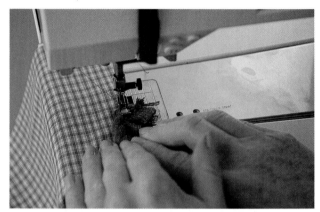

STEP 2 * Place the flat edge of the cording along the raw edges of the project. Arrange the raw ends of the cording so they hang off the raw edge of the fabric. Start your stitching on a side, not at a corner.

STEP 3 * Use a zipper foot to baste the cording in place. The zipper foot will allow you to stitch right next to the cording.

STEP 4 * When you get to a corner, clip the flat part of the cording edge, right to the cord, so it will go around the corner without bunching up.

STEP 5 * When you get to the end, cut the cording so you have a little overlap. Unravel the ends again, and arrange the raw ends of the cording so they drape over the raw edges of the fabric.

STEP 6 * Pin the back of the project to the front, and stitch around the project, leaving an opening for turning and inserting a pillow form (if this is for a pillow).

Dry Brushing

Painting techniques are not often included in quilting books, but adding cheek color to the characters on the quilts is essential to the look of the project. In the old days, you just reached in your purse, dragged out your blush, and applied it to the cheeks—yours and the doll's. Acrylic paint offers a better range of colors and permanence.

STEP 1 * Use a stiff brush, a traditional stencil brush, or an old "scrubby" one. The brush I like best is a little nylon brush that has a little stiffness to it.

STEP 2 * Dip the brush into the paint color, and rub the brush onto a piece of paper towel until the paint begins to have a powder-like look.

STEP 3 * Gently, and in a circular motion, apply the brush to the fabric, and keep brushing the color on until you get the depth of color you desire. Use a dry iron with a pressing cloth to heat-set the color if you plan to wash the quilt.

Antiquing Fabric Using Paint and Water

There are few people who aren't charmed by the look of old things, and we try valiantly to recreate that look. There are new products that have increased our ability to achieve that look. The flag that is stitched onto the "Miss Liberty" quilt has been sprayed with glossy wood tone (this product can be found in craft stores in the floral spray section). To achieve the antique look on dolls and wall quilts; you can use the method below, which gives just the right touch.

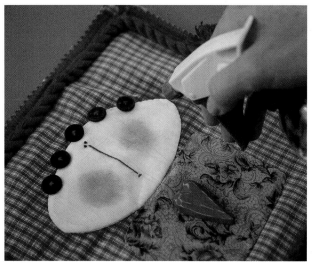

STEP 1 * Spray the area to be antiqued (face and hands) with water.

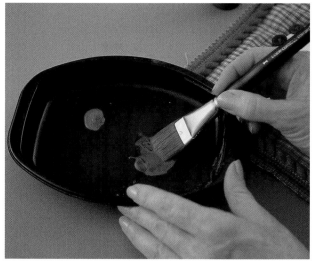

STEP 2 * Mix any brand of raw umber acrylic paint with water. The proportions just have to be experimental—but there is more water than paint in the mixture. If the color isn't dark enough, add more paint.

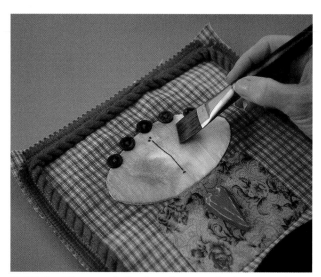

STEP 3 * Use a soft flat brush to apply the water/paint mixture to the area to be antiqued.

STEP 4 * Let the project dry thoroughly. If you need to add another layer, spray with water first.

Embroidery Stitches

Basic embroidery stitches add lovely accents to all your quilting and sewing projects. Follow the simple steps below, and you'll be on your way to becoming an accomplished stitcher.

Note: *When you pull the strand from a package of embroidery floss, you will find a strand contains six threads. Check the instructions for how many threads to use for each project.*

Stem stitch

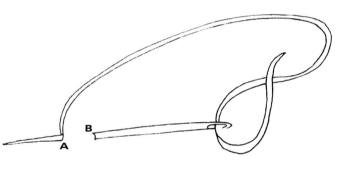

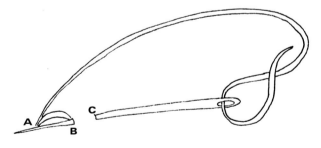

STEP 1 * Come up at A, down at B, then exit at A.

STEP 2 * Insert needle into C, then exit from B.

STEP 3 * Continue this sequence to stitch a line.

The stems from the lobelias are stem stitched.

STEP 1 * Bring knotted thread up at A.

STEP 2 * Wrap the thread around the needle three or four times.

STEP 3 * Re-enter the needle into A, pulling the thread slightly, as you pull the needle downward.

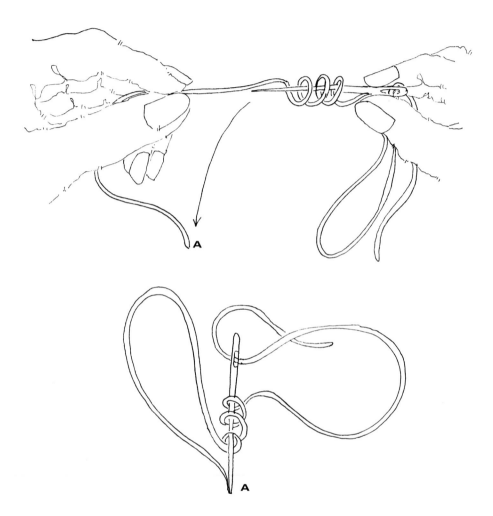

French knot centers accentuate the pansy.

Running stitch

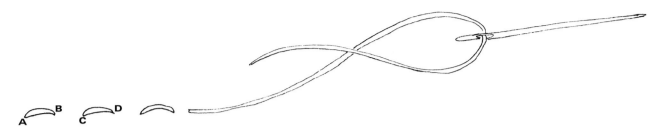

STEP 1 * Bring the needle up at A, down at B, up at C, down at D, and so forth.

The running stitch surrounds the star.

Feather Stitch

STEP 1 * Bring the needle up at A, down at B, up through C, catching the A-B thread, and down at D.

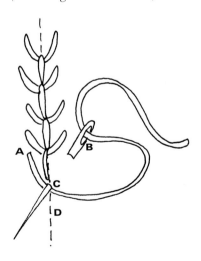

The feather stitch creates a laced look on the Horse Pillow.

STEP 1 * Bring the needle up at A, over on a diagonal to B, up through C, and repeat this sequence.

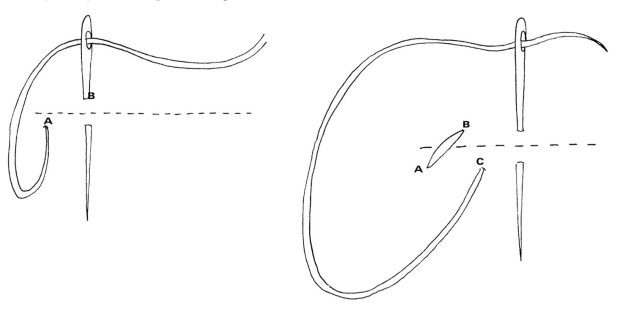

The Buffalo Pillow background is whipstitched to the border fabric.

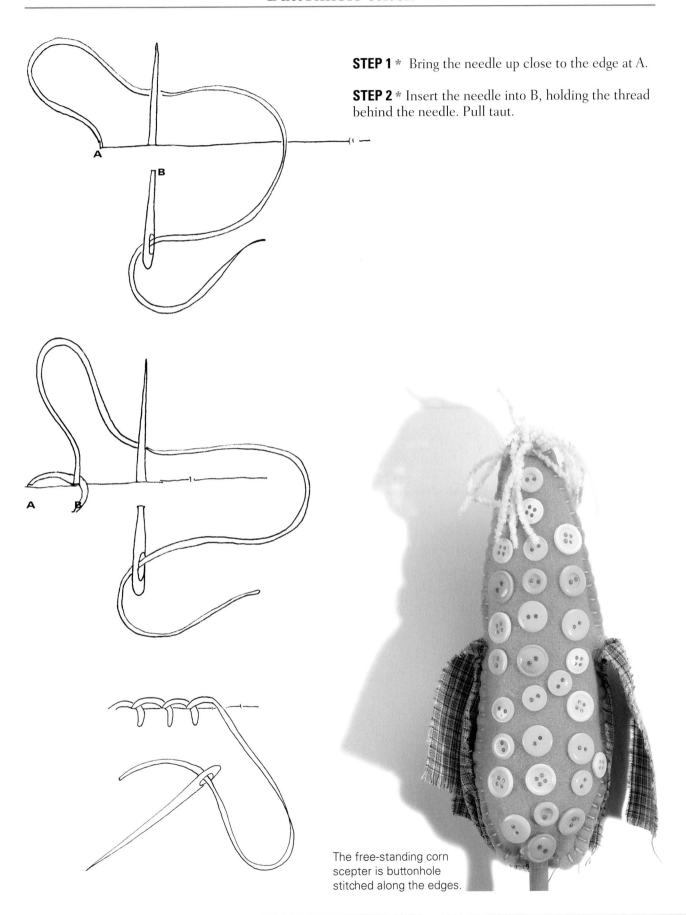

STEP 1 * Bring the needle up close to the edge at A.

STEP 2 * Insert the needle into B, holding the thread behind the needle. Pull taut.

The free-standing corn scepter is buttonhole stitched along the edges.

STEP 1 * To make a flower, bring the needle up at the center (A).

STEP 2 * Reinsert the needle into the center, exiting about ¼" or more from the center (B). Keep the thread behind the needle.

STEP 3 * Make a small stitch at the top of the loop (C) to keep it in place. Do not pull the loop too tight. Exit from (A) to create more petals. Exit further down the stem to create leaves.

Note: *You can use the same technique along a stem to create leaves.*

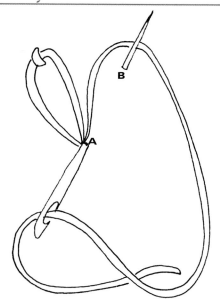

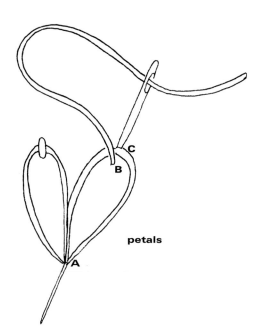

petals

The branches on the Shaker Tree of Life, page 86, use the lazy daisy stitch.

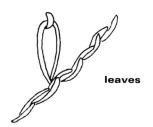

leaves

Straight Stitch

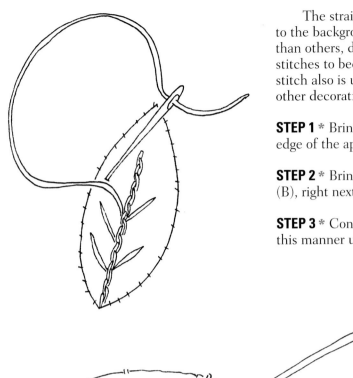

The straight stitch is used to appliqué the pieces to the background. Some of the stitches are longer than others, depending on whether you want the stitches to become part of the design. The straight stitch also is useful for making veins in leaves or other decorative accents.

STEP 1 * Bring the needle and thread up close to the edge of the appliqué (A).

STEP 2 * Bring the needle to the background fabric (B), right next to the appliqué piece.

STEP 3 * Continue all the way around the piece in this manner until it is attached to the background.

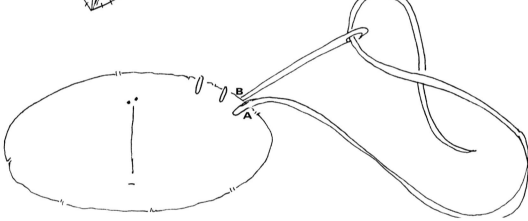

The apples from the Shaker Proverb, page 80, are good examples of the straight stitch.

This is a silk-ribbon embroidery method, which I adapted for Ruth Ellen's Quilt (page 52).

STEP 1 * Tear the red marbled fabric into 1" x 45" strips (about one strip for each rose).

STEP 2 * Place the quilt block in an embroidery hoop. Using a full strand of embroidery floss with a knotted end, come up in the center of the quilt block (A) and down about 2½" from the center (B).

STEP 3 * Bring the thread up again and form a figure that resembles a wagon wheel with just the spokes— no rim. There will be a total of five spokes.

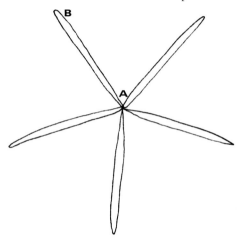

STEP 4 * Exit the needle and thread below, and tie a knot. Do not cut the thread; just let it dangle there for a minute.

STEP 5 * Thread a large darning needle with the torn strip of fabric. It is often easier to thread if you cut the fabric end at a diagonal.

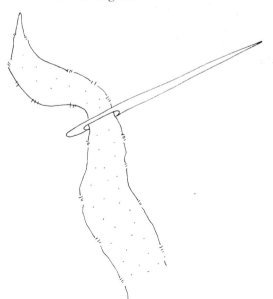

STEP 6 * Use a needle and floss to take a stitch to secure the opposite end of the fabric strip to the center of the spokes. Make a knot again on the wrong side, and let the needle dangle.

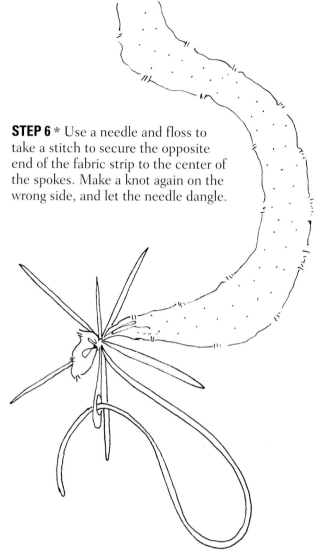

STEP 7 * Work in a counter-clockwise direction and take the fabric under the first spoke, over the next, just like weaving a basket.

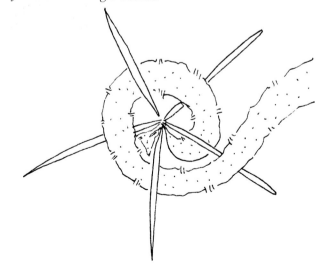

STEP 8 * Continue the over-under sequence, twisting the fabric a little as you go. Work from the center outward. The rose will begin to form, but don't pull the fabric too tight.

STEP 9 * When the fabric covers the embroidery floss adequately, cut the fabric, and tuck the raw edge under the edge of the rose.

STEP 10 * Use the needle and floss to stitch the flower on the wrong side of the block. Stitch in several places to keep it in place.

wrong side

Yo-yos and Tassels

Tassels and yo-yos are quick and easy embellishments to perk up your projects. Yo-yos can be used for buttons, punky hair on a doll, or anything with a circular look, and tassels make great hair. Use your imagination, and you'll discover a variety of ways to use both of these techniques.

Yo-yos

STEP 1 * To make a yo-yo, cut a circle from the fabric. Use a pattern or follow the size guide in the instructions.

STEP 2 * Make a running stitch around the edge of the fabric, about ⅛" from the raw edge of the circle.

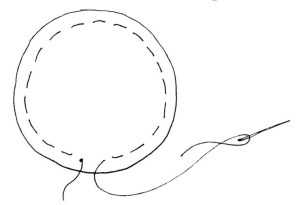

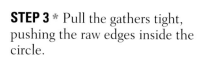

STEP 3 * Pull the gathers tight, pushing the raw edges inside the circle.

STEP 4 * Make a knot, then use the yo-yos to embellish your quilt or pillow.

Tassels

STEP 1 * Cut lengths of yarn.

STEP 2 * Tie the yarn in the center with another piece of yarn.

STEP 3 * Trim, if needed.

STEP 4 * Glue to the top of corn, doll's head, etc.

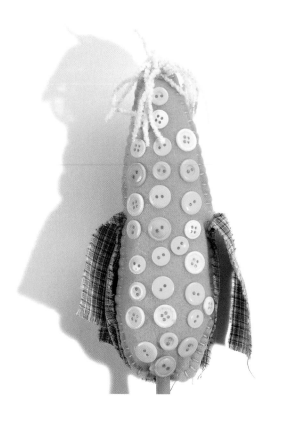

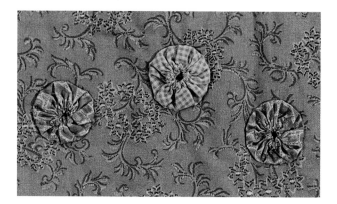

Machine Quilting

A few years ago, I was introduced to the joys of machine quilting. Until that moment, I was one of those who snubbed anything like a tied quilt or one that wasn't stitched by hand. That was one area in which I felt I was a purist. Now I realize the folly of that way of thinking. For one thing, it really ties up the number of quilts I can produce. For another thing, most people don't care. They just love to touch the machine stippled quilts and feel the texture of all the swirls. Here's how I do it:

STEP 1 * Prepare your machine by dropping the feed dogs and attaching your darning foot. Thread the machine with your chosen thread. There are special quilting threads for machine quilting.

Before dropping feed dogs

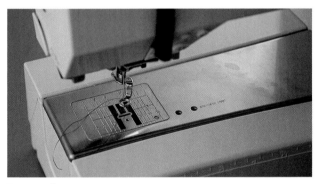

Darning foot

After dropping feed dogs

STEP 2 * Place the quilt onto the machine, and take two or three stitches in the same place to get started. Place the needle in the "down" position as you quilt. *Note: I find it easier to guide the machine when I use little latex finger gloves; it grips the fabric better.*

STEP 3 * As you press the foot pedal, guide the needle in little swirl patterns, moving from one area of the quilt top to the next. I sometimes leave the main "picture" in the quilt unquilted, and just quilt all the background.

STEP 4 * When you are finished, trim all the threads and bind the quilt.

SPRING

When January comes, with its dreary skies and cold weather, I start dreaming of spring. Of course, that doesn't really happen for a few more months, but when I see the little crocuses come up, the forsythia start to explode yellow blossoms and the tulips in bloom, I'm in heaven. Yes, I know allergy season starts, but I sniffle with a smile on my face! The spring sunshine lifts my spirits and gives me energy. Like the Buffalo Gals, who dance by the light of the moon, I dance out in the yard with my rake. I go to the store to buy some of those little cotton gloves, which wear out in a week but come in great colors! You will see evidence of my love of spring when you see the quilts in this section—and one even sports those little garden gloves!

Finished size 69" x 89"

Buffalo Gals, Won't You Come Out to Dance?

My dad used to entertain us children by singing silly songs. *"Oh, My Darlin' Clementine"*, *"Nellie Blye"* and *"Buffalo Gals"* were some of my favorites. Both my parents sang to us, but Daddy's tunes were usually funny and folksy, while Mama's were beautiful and melodic. *"Buffalo Gals"* had a particular appeal, because I envisioned girls in colorful dresses with funny buffalo hats on their heads, dancing around a fire by the light of the moon. Anything done by the light of the moon has the possibility of being fun!

materials

2⅛ yd. dark blue flannel for background squares
⅞ yd. dark blue print fabric for sashing around squares
⅓ yd. muslin for arms and heads
⅛ yd. each of two different browns for trunks
Assorted fat quarters and scraps for clothing, stars, moon, trees
1 yd. dark bright blue fabric for tree border
1 yd. each of eight bright colors for the flying geese border
3 yd. midnight blue fabric for the flying geese border **Note:** 1½ yd. of two different blue prints may be used for the flying geese border
Embroidery floss: dark brown, light coral, antique gold, tan
Funky yarns for hair
Scrap of gold felt for horns on hat
1¼ yd. brown flannel for binding
6½ yd. for quilt backing
Full-size cotton batting (81" x 96")
Acrylic paint: terra cotta

cutting instructions

STEP 1 * Using the patterns from the pattern insert, trace, stitch, trim seam allowance, and complete four Buffalo Gal faces and eight hands from the muslin, following the directions for Double Appliqué on pages 8 and 9.

STEP 2 * Using the patterns from the pattern insert, trace, stitch, trim seam allowance, and complete the clothing, stars, moon and trees, following the directions for Double Appliqué on pages 8 and 9.

STEP 3 * Cut 16 squares (12") from the dark blue flannel.

STEP 4 * Cut 11 strips (2½" x 45") from the dark blue print. Sew all the strips together end to end. From these cut eight strips (2½" x 12"), four strips (2½" x 25½"), and three strips (2½" x 52½").

STEP 5 * Cut four strips (9" x 45") from the bright blue fabric.

STEP 6 * Cut one strip (2½" x 45") from one of the brown fabrics.

STEP 7 * Cut one strip (1¼" x 45") from the other brown fabric.

STEP 8 * Cut seven strips (14½" x 9½") from each of the eight bright colors.

STEP 9 * Cut 20 strips (5" x 45") from the midnight blue fabric.

gals assembly

STEP 1 * Stitch the Gals and their clothing using the Double Appliqué method on pages 8 and 9.

STEP 2 * Refer to the stitch instructions on pages 19-25 for all embroidery. Use two threads to embroider the faces. Use dark brown to French knot the eyes and tan to stem stitch the nose. With light coral floss stitch two straight stitches on top of each other for the mouth.

STEP 3 * Dry brush the cheeks, using terra cotta acrylic paint. See Dry Brushing, page 17.

quilt center assembly

STEP 1 * For the background, sew two 12" squares of the flannel together with the dark blue print strips in between the squares. Make eight (12" x 25½").

STEP 2 * Sew two sets of squares together with a dark blue sashing strip in between them. Make four (25½" x 25½").

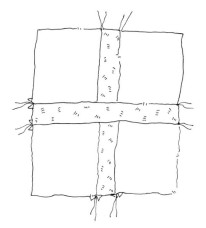

STEP 3 * Sew the two rows of squares together with a dark blue sashing strip in between them and on the top and bottom. This will form the large central section of your quilt (52½" x 56½").

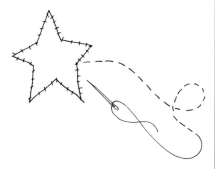

STEP 4 * Hand appliqué the Buffalo Gals and the stars onto the squares.

STEP 5 * Using the antique gold floss (two strands), make running stitches to form star trails near each star.

STEP 6 * Embroider the moon, and dry brush the moon cheeks. Stitch the moon to the center of the squares using the straight stitch.

tree borders

STEP 1 ✳ Sew together the four (9" x 45") strips of bright blue. Cut two borders the width of the quilt.

STEP 2 ✳ Make the tree trunks. Sew the 2½" x 45" strip with right sides together along the long edge. Turn right-side out. Press with the seam to the back. Repeat with the second brown strip.

STEP 3 ✳ Segment cut the trunks in varying lengths so some of the trees are taller than others. See the pattern insert for sample sizes.

STEP 4 ✳ Appliqué the trees and trunks across the 9" strips (seven large trees, six small trees). Arrange the trees so the sizes and height vary, and group three trees together next to lone trees.

STEP 5 ✳ With right sides together, stitch one border to the top of the quilt and the other to the bottom. Press seam allowances toward the borders.

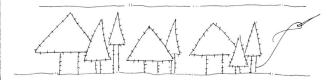

flying geese border

STEP 1 ✳ The outer border is a very casual version of "Flying Geese." To make each strip, you will use the 14½" x 9½" strips from eight different colors. Stack four different colors together and use your rotary cutter to cut them in four pieces; don't cut nice, little, equal pieces. Make the lines less than the standard 90-degree angle. Arrange each set of four colors so all four colors are shown next to each other.

STEP 2 * Place the midnight blue fabric strips over the first color block to create the first side of the triangle (the main color being the center).

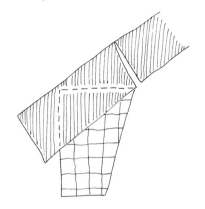

STEP 3 * Trim off one end, then turn the midnight blue so the fabrics are right sides together. *Note: You will have to scoot the fabric down about ¼" to accommodate the seam allowance.*

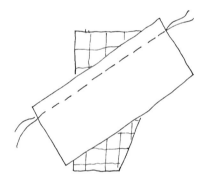

STEP 4 * Sew the blue fabric to the print.

STEP 5 * Press the midnight blue fabric up, and trim to fit the original block.

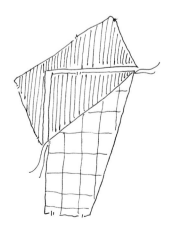

STEP 6 * Trim off the main color from the back of the midnight blue fabric.

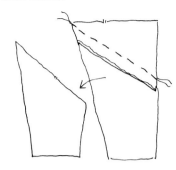

STEP 7 * Repeat Steps 2-6 for the other side of the triangle.

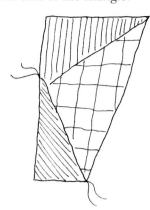

STEP 8 * Repeat for all four colors, and sew the blocks together so they fit together as originally cut.

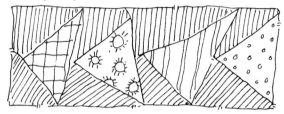

STEP 9 * Repeat this entire procedure for the other four colors, and stitch the borders together, alternating color combinations 1 and 2.

STEP 10 * The borders all have the apex of the triangles going the same way. Start on the right side, with five sets of four, stitched end to end. Trim off excess. (18 triangles)

STEP 11 * The top is next, with four sets of four. Trim off excess. (15 triangles)

STEP 12 * The left side is five sets of four. (20 triangles)

STEP 13 * The bottom is five sets of four. Trim the excess. (18 triangles)

quilt assembly

Assemble and bind the quilt, following the instructions on pages 12-15.

Finished Size: 33½" tall

Buffalo Gal Doll

As many of you know, I have written several doll-making books, and I rather enjoy the fun you can have making dolls. This little girl can be adapted to be anyone you want her to be, including any of the other people depicted on the quilts in this book. Just change her clothing, add some amazing little embellishments, and voila!

materials

¼ yd. tea-dyed muslin for head, arms, body, hat and lining
½ yd. check print for bloomers
½ yd. large print for dress and sleeves
⅓ yd. striped print for apron
Fat quarter for gloves
Assorted scraps for boots, legs and bow
5" crocheted doily for collar
Stuffing
Funky yarn for hair
Scrap of fur for hat
Scrap of gold felt for horns
Embroidery floss: dark brown, tan, light coral, and a color to match the clothing
Decorative button for collar
4 buttons (⅝") for cuffs
Small flag
Acrylic paint: terra cotta

cutting instructions

Note: These patterns include seam allowances.

STEP 1 * Using the patterns from the pattern insert, trace, and cut out the hat, head and arms from a double piece of muslin. Cut a third head piece.

STEP 2 * Using the patterns from the pattern insert, cut out the legs, gloves, cuffs and boots from three appropriate fabrics.

STEP 3 * Using the pattern from the pattern insert, cut out the hat from the fur scrap.

STEP 4 * Using the pattern from the pattern insert, cut out four horns from the gold felt.

STEP 5 * Cut two 5" x 8" body pieces from a double piece of muslin.

STEP 6 * Tear two pieces (15" x 14") of the bloomer fabric.

STEP 7 * Tear one piece (16" x 30") of the dress fabric.

STEP 8 * Tear two pieces (7" x 13") of the sleeve fabric.

STEP 9 * Tear one piece (12" x 30") of the apron fabric.

head assembly

Note: All seam allowances are ¼".

STEP 1 * Trace the features and embroider the face on two layers of the muslin head piece. Using two threads for all embroidery, make two French knot eyes; stem stitch the nose with tan floss; and make two straight stitches for the mouth. Refer to the stitch instructions on pages 19-25.

STEP 2 * Place the head pieces right sides together. Stitch around the head, leaving a 3" opening at the top for turning.

STEP 3 * Turn right side out, and stuff firmly. Stitch the opening closed.

STEP 4 * Dry brush the cheeks per instructions on page 17.

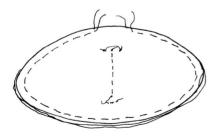

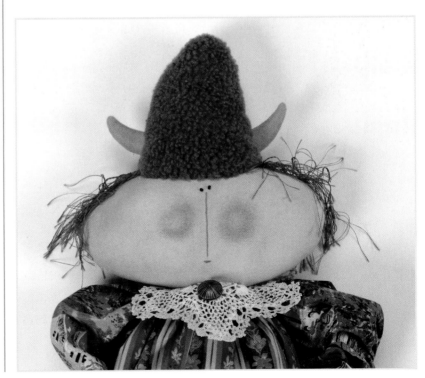

body assembly

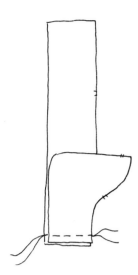

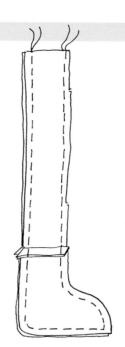

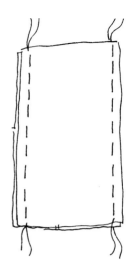

STEP 1 * With right sides together, stitch a boot to the leg. Press toward the boot. Repeat for all four leg pieces.

STEP 2 * Place two legs right sides together, and stitch, leaving an opening at the top. Turn right-side out, and stuff up to within 1" of the knee line. Topstitch across the leg, and continue stuffing to within 1" of the top. Repeat for other leg.

STEP 3 * With right sides together, stitch the sides of the body. Leave top and bottom ends open.

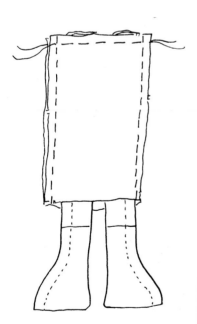

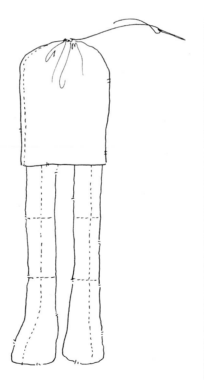

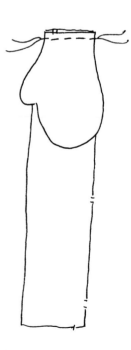

STEP 4 * Place the legs inside the body tube so the raw edges of the legs are even with the raw edges of the body tube. Stitch across, and turn right side out.

STEP 5 * Stuff the body firmly, and gather the top edge, poking the raw edges inside as you pull the gathers tight. Make a knot.

STEP 6 * With right sides together, stitch the glove to the arm. Press toward the glove. Repeat for all four arm pieces.

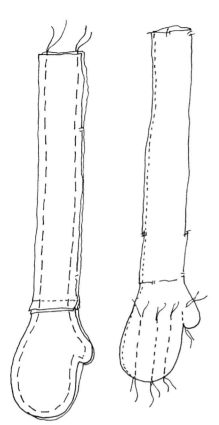

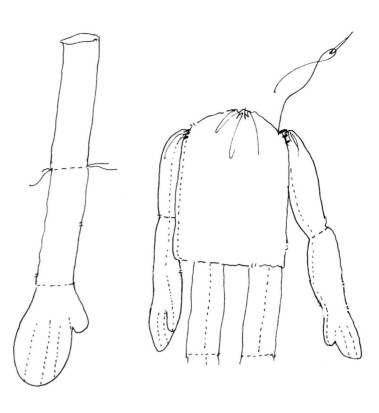

STEP 7 * With right sides together, stitch the two arm pieces together, leaving an opening at the top of the arm. Clip the corners, turn right-side out, and topstitch the fingers.

STEP 8 * Carefully insert small pieces of stuffing into each finger cavity, pushing gently with a stuffing tool or small dowel. Stuff the arm to within 1" of the elbow line, then topstitch. Continue stuffing to within 1" of the top. Turn the raw edges inside, and stitch the arm to the shoulder. Repeat for other arm.

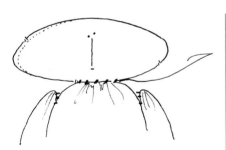

STEP 9 * Pin the head to the top of the body, and stitch firmly in place.

STEP 10 * Place the glove cuff pieces right sides together. Stitch, leaving the bottom (smaller curve) open. Turn right side out, and press.

STEP 11 * Stitch two buttons to the side of the glove cuff, and overlap the cuff around the top of the hand seam. Glue in place.

STEP 12 * Tear a strip of fabric 1" wide, and wrap around the glove cuff to hide the raw ends. Tie in a square knot and trim the ends at an angle. Add a small amount of glue to keep from slipping.

STEP 13 * If desired, antique the doll using the method described on page 18.

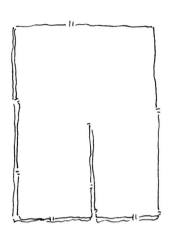

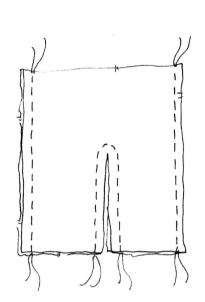

STEP 1 * Take the 15" x 14" bloomer pieces. The 14" edges are the sides of the bloomers. Cut an 11½" slit for the inseam.

STEP 2 * With right sides together, stitch the sides and inseam. Clip the inseam to the stitching, and then turn right-side out. Press.

STEP 3 * Gather the top edge of the bloomers with some matching embroidery floss. Place the bloomers on the doll. Pull the gathers tight, and then knot the thread.

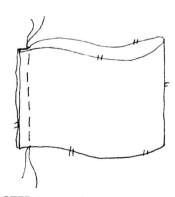

STEP 4 * For the dress, stitch the two 16" edges, right sides together. Press them open, and turn right-side out.

STEP 5 * Gather the top edge and place just under the arms of the doll. Pull the gathers tight, and make a knot.

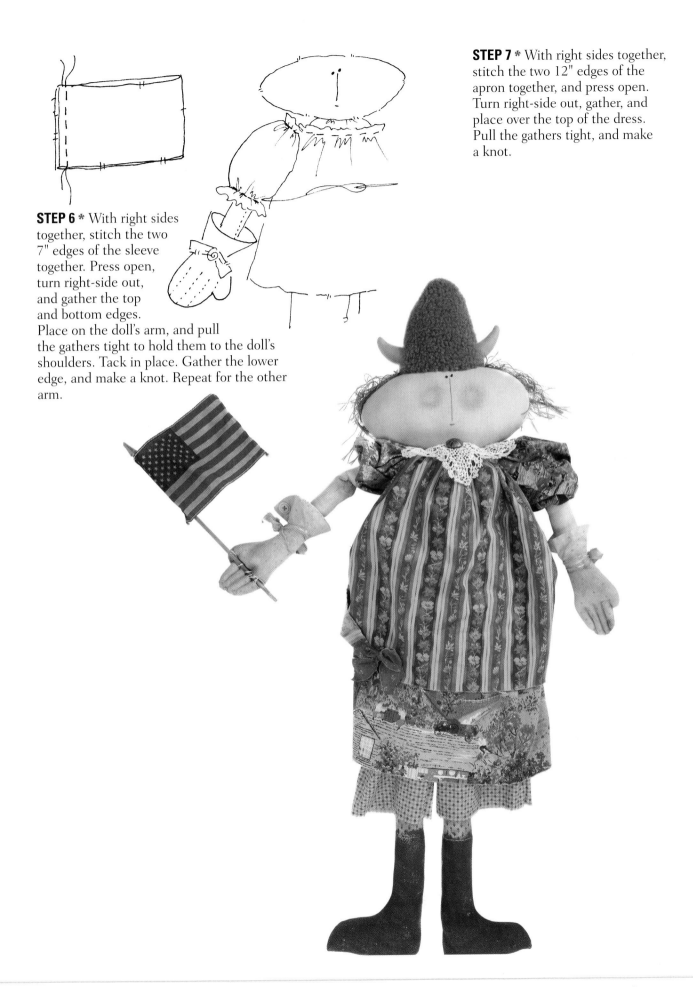

STEP 7 * With right sides together, stitch the two 12" edges of the apron together, and press open. Turn right-side out, gather, and place over the top of the dress. Pull the gathers tight, and make a knot.

STEP 6 * With right sides together, stitch the two 7" edges of the sleeve together. Press open, turn right-side out, and gather the top and bottom edges. Place on the doll's arm, and pull the gathers tight to hold them to the doll's shoulders. Tack in place. Gather the lower edge, and make a knot. Repeat for the other arm.

accessories and embellishments

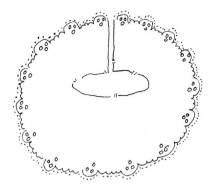

STEP 1 * Cut a neck opening into the lace doily, and glue to the doll's neck to cover the raw edges of the dress and apron.

STEP 2 * Glue the decorative button on the collar.

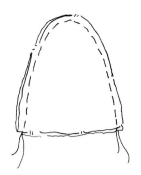

STEP 3 * With right sides together, sew the hat pieces together. Turn right-side out.

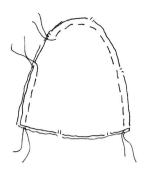

STEP 4 * Stitch the muslin lining pieces together, leaving a slit for turning.
Note: *The lining is to keep the hat from stretching when you stuff it.*

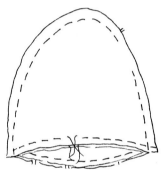

STEP 5 * Place the hat and lining right sides together, and stitch the lower edges together. Turn right-side out through the lining, and stitch the lining opening closed.

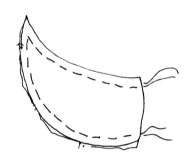

STEP 6 * Stitch the felt horns together, leaving the bottom open. Trim the seam allowance, and turn right-side out.

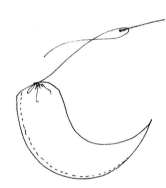

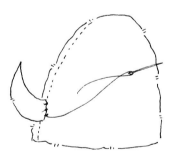

STEP 7 * Stuff the horns. Gather the open end, and stitch to the side of the hat, at the seam, 1" above the lower edge.

STEP 8 * Stuff the hat lightly, and stitch to the doll's head.

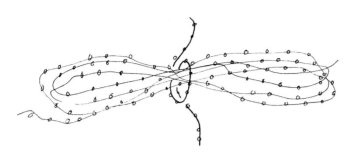

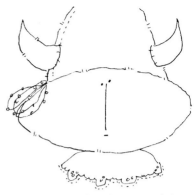

STEP 9 * Loop six lengths of funky yarn, each 8" long. Tie loops in the middle with another piece of yarn.

STEP 10 * Glue to the side of the hat, draping along the seam line of the doll's head. Repeat for other side of head.

STEP 11 * If you like, you can antique a flag (refer to the instructions on page 18), and stitch it to the inside of the doll's hand.

STEP 12 * Add a bow to the lower edge of the apron if you like—tear a 1" strip of contrasting fabric, and stitch in place.

Finished Size: 14" x 14"

Buffalo Pillow

The Buffalo nickel is something I can actually remember—yes, I am ancient. I have always felt sad that their numbers were decimated, and there was so much wanton killing of these magnificent beasts. Fortunately, people have begun to wake up, and we still are able to see a few left. Here's my tribute to the noble animal, and the way I imagine life must have been when their numbers were great.

materials

Fat quarter of the following fabrics:
Dark brown felt for buffalo
Honey brown flannel for background
Blanket fabric for borders
Backing fabric
Scrap of tan felt for buffalo horns
Embroidery floss: tomato red
1⅓ yd. cording edging
12" pillow form

cutting instructions

STEP 1 * Using the patterns from the pattern insert, cut the buffalo and horn from the felt fabric.

STEP 2 * Cut a 10" square from the honey brown fabric.

STEP 3 * Cut four strips (2½") from the border fabric. From these cut two top and bottom borders (2½" x 10"), and two side borders (2½" x 14").

STEP 4 * Cut a 14" square from the backing fabric.

pillow top piecing

STEP 1 * Refer to the stitch instructions on pages 19-25 for all embroidery. Hand appliqué the buffalo and his horn to the center of the honey brown flannel using the straight stitch.

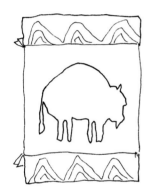

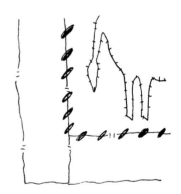

STEP 2 * With right sides together, stitch the top and bottom borders (2½" x 10") to the background, and press toward the borders.

STEP 3 * Add the side borders, and press toward the borders.

STEP 4 * Use the tomato red floss (two strands) to whipstitch the juncture of the border and background.

pillow assembly

STEP 1 * Attach the cording edging to the pillow top, per the instructions on page 16.

STEP 2 * With right sides together, stitch the pillow top and backing together, leaving one side open. Turn right-side out.

STEP 3 * Insert the pillow form, and stitch the opening closed.

See page 102 for the Horse Pillow instructions.

Finished Size: 39" square

Harewood Forest

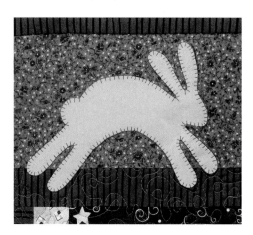

I wished for many years that I could visit Europe, and especially England. Several years ago, I finally was able to go to England for 10 glorious days. As I drove through the English countryside with my friends, I was charmed by the names of the roads, forests and even the cottages along the way. One evening at dusk, we came to a stop on the roadway. I looked up at a small hill and saw a sign reading "Harewood Forest." I thought that was a very sweet name, but just then, I noticed a group of rabbits come out of their holes to dance and cavort in their joyous greeting to the evening. That was the most perfect ending to a day that I can remember. It just made me laugh to see it.

materials

- ⅓ yd. blue fabric for the background
- ¼ yd. dark blue print fabric for the inner sashings
- ⅔ yd. maroon print fabric for the sashings and binding
- ¾ yd. olive green print fabric for the borders
- 3 fat quarters of coordinating prints for the stars and windmills
- Fat quarter yellow print fabric for the cornerstones
- 1⅓ yd. backing fabric
- ⅓ yd. maroon print binding fabric
- 45" x 45" piece of thin cotton batting
- 24" x 20" black wool felt
- 12" x 20" tan wool felt
- Quilting thread: black, rust

cutting instructions

STEP 1 * Using the patterns from the pattern insert, trace, stitch, trim seam allowance, and complete two windmills, two windmill centers, two large stars and two small stars using the Double Appliqué method on pages 8 and 9, and the appropriate fabrics.

STEP 2 * Cut four squares (9½") from the blue fabric.

STEP 3 * Cut 16 squares (2") from the yellow print.

STEP 4 * Cut four strips (2" x 45") from the dark blue print. From these cut 16 strips (2 x 9½") for the borders.

STEP 5 * Cut six strips (2" x 45") and four strips (2½" x 45") from the maroon fabric. From the 2" strips, cut two strips (2" x 12½"), three strips (2" x 26"), and two strips (2" x 29"). The 2" strips are for the sashings; the 2½" strips are for the binding.

STEP 6 * Cut four strips (6" x 45") from the olive green fabric.

STEP 7 * Cut one square (45" x 45") for the backing.

STEP 8 * Cut out seven black rabbits and four tan rabbits from the wool felt.

block assembly

STEP 1 * Sew the windmills and stars, and assemble them according to the Double Appliqué instructions on pages 8 and 9. Stitch the finished appliqués to the blue 9½" background squares. Embellish the center of each windmill with a yo-yo (see page 28) made from a 3½" circle.

STEP 2 * Assemble the background squares by adding a dark blue print sashing strip to opposite sides of the blue 9½" squares.

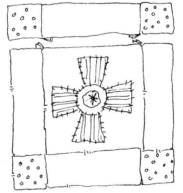

STEP 3 * Stitch a yellow square to each end of the eight remaining sashing strips. Attach these to the top and bottom of the four background blocks (12½" x 12½").

quilt top piecing

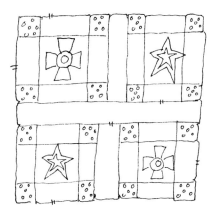

STEP 1 * Assemble the top row of the quilt center by alternating a windmill block/maroon sashing strip (2" x 12½")/star block. Reverse the order for the bottom row (12½" x 26").

STEP 2 * Sew the two rows together with a maroon sashing (2" x 26") strip in between them (26" x 26").

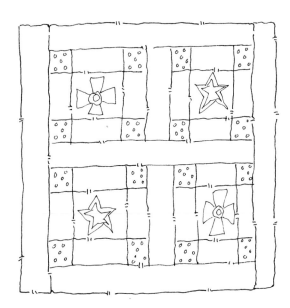

STEP 3 * Attach maroon sashing strips (2" x 26") to the top and bottom, and then attach the side sashing strips (2" x 29").

STEP 4 * Attach the top and bottom olive borders (6" x 29"), then the sides (6" x 40").

STEP 5 * Appliqué the rabbits in a random pattern on the green border.

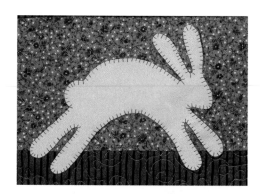

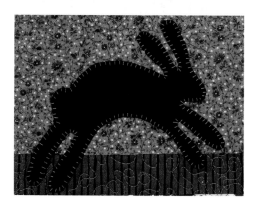

quilt assembly

STEP 1 * Assemble the quilt and binding per the instructions on pages 12-15.

STEP 2 * The center blocks are all machine stippled using olive green thread (see stippling, page 29).

Finished size: 70½" x 82"

Ruth Ellen's Red and White Quilt

I remember falling in love with the colors red and white when I rode in my cousin Jeffrey's new car. His mom picked us up to go swimming (this was early grade school days), and they had a new Ford station wagon. The outside was a very soft gray and white, but the inside was great! The ceiling was white, but there were tiny holes that exposed some sort of red lining underneath. Tiny polka dots! The leather seats were bright red, and so was the padded dash. All the carpet and door panels were soft gray, with a lot of chrome trim. Since I was a child of the '50s, this was also reminiscent of the wonderful old soda fountains. This quilt is a tribute to those days, and Ruth Ellen's wonderful Ford station wagon.

materials

⅓ yd. white fabric for center block squares
1 yd. red/white windowpane check fabric for blocks
1 yd. red/white toile fabric for blocks
⅓ yd. red/white ticking fabric for blocks
¼ yd. of each of the following fabrics for blocks:
Celery green print
Red/white small floral print
Celery/red/white print
White/red paisley
Dark red print
Medium red print
⅔ yd. medium red marbled print fabric for the roses
⅓ yd. celery green marbled print fabric for the leaves
1½ yd. red/white rosebud print fabric for the sashing
1⅓ yd. green floral print fabric for the borders
1⅓ yd. red print fabric for the binding
5½ yd. backing fabric
78" x 90" piece of thin cotton batting
Embroidery floss: red, medium green
8½ yd. large red rickrack

cutting instructions

Make 15 of each block.

STEP 1 * Using the pattern from the pattern insert, trace, and cut 30 triangles from the toile and 30 triangles from the windowpane check.

STEP 2 * From the white fabric, cut 15 squares (5½").

STEP 3 * From the red/white ticking, cut two strips (3" x 45"). Cut so the stripes are vertical.

STEP 4 * Cut 15 squares (3") from each of the following fabrics: red/white windowpane check, celery print, red/white small floral print.

STEP 5 * From the celery/red/white print, cut three strips (2" x 45"). These are for the top of the square, which will touch the windowpane check.

STEP 6 * From the white/red paisley, cut three strips (2" x 45").

STEP 7 * From the dark red print, cut three strips (1½" x 45").

STEP 8 * From the medium red print, cut three strips (1½" x 45").

STEP 9 * From the red/white rosebud print, cut 14 strips (3½" x 45") for the sashing strips.

STEP 10 * From the border fabric, cut seven strips (5" x 45").

STEP 11 * From the binding fabric, cut nine strips (5" x 45") for the binding.

triangle blocks – make 15

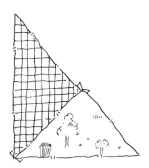

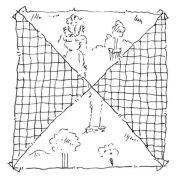

STEP 1 * Sew a toile triangle to a windowpane triangle, right sides together, from the apex to the base as shown. Press the seams open.

STEP 2 * With right sides together, sew two of the assembled triangle pieces together as shown.

rose blocks - make 15

The rose block is a modified log cabin block with the sides attached in a counter-clockwise direction. Watch the illustrations closely for fabric placement.

STEP 1 * Place the white square, right sides together, on top of the ticking strip. Sew the seam.

STEP 2 * Without cutting the ticking strip, add another block next to the first, and continue stitching each block until all of the white squares have a ticking strip attached to one side.

STEP 3 * Use your cutting mat and ruler to cut between all of the blocks and square them off.

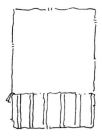

STEP 4 * Press the seam allowance toward the ticking strip.
Note: *All seam allowances should be pressed away from the center block.*

STEP 5 * Take the 3" squares cut from the red/white windowpane check, celery print, and red/white small print. With right sides together, sew the windowpane check and the red/white small print to opposite sides of the celery print squares. Make 15 strips.

STEP 6 * Sew a strip of three squares (from Step 5) to the left side of the block, placing the red/white small print next to the ticking strip.

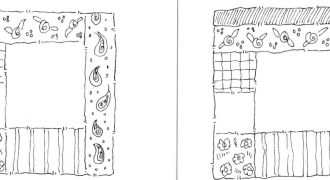

STEP 7 * Continue around the block in the same manner, attaching the celery/red print and then the white/red paisley.

STEP 8 * The dark red print strip is sewn above the celery/red print.

STEP 9 * The final strip, the medium red print, is sewn to the white/red paisley.

STEP 10 * Using the medium red marbled print, create the roses in the center of the rose blocks, following the instructions for the Modified Spider Rose on page 26.

STEP 11 * Prepare one to three leaves per rose block (no more than 25 total), using the Double Appliqué instructions on pages 8 and 9, and the pattern from the pattern insert.

STEP 12 * Refer to the stitch instructions, pages 19-25. Embroider the leaf pattern with one thread of medium green floss using the stem stitch.

STEP 13 * Use the straight stitch in a matching thread color to attach the leaf to the block.

sashing and border piecing

STEP 1 * Sew the red/white rosebud sashing strips together, end to end. Press the seams open.

STEP 2 * Sew the border strips together, end to end. Press the seams open.

STEP 3 * Sew the binding strips together, end to end. Press the seams open.

quilt top piecing

STEP 1 * Arrange the blocks on the floor in a checkerboard pattern.

STEP 2 * With right sides together, stitch a piece of sashing between all the vertical sides. Do not put sashing on the outside edges yet. Press the seam allowances toward the sashing.

STEP 3 * With right sides together, attach the horizontal sashing strips. Pin carefully before you stitch to avoid uneven sashing and blocks.

STEP 4 * Add sashing strips to the sides, top and bottom of the quilt.

STEP 5 * Attach the border strips to the side's top, and bottom of the quilt.

STEP 6 * Stitch large red rickrack to inside edges of the border.

quilt assembly

STEP 1 * Layer, quilt and bind the quilt following the instructions on pages 12-15.

STEP 2 * The quilt shown was machine stippled over the entire surface.

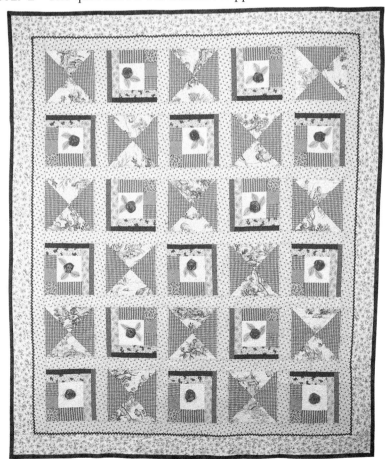

Finished Size: 46½" x 46½"

Mama's Flower Garden

This little quilt honors my own mama, who always surrounds herself with bursts of color in her yard. When my parents moved from the farm into the house they built in town, the first priority became the flowers and grass in the yard. Every little corner has something blooming. I think my parents miss Old Crow Farm, but they truly have learned to bloom where they are planted. Like my mama's yard, you can go through your cupboard, glean a few little scraps of color and put them together for everyone to enjoy.

materials

- ½ yd. light gray print fabric for center blocks
- ⅛ yd. of 9 different floral fabrics (or scraps) for block borders
- Scraps for flowers
- 1¼ yd. medium green print fabric for the sashing/outer borders
- ⅓ yd. dark medium green print fabric for the binding
- 50" x 50" piece of thin cotton batting
- Assorted cloth gardening gloves (old or new)
- 4 skeins of medium green embroidery floss for quilted accents around each block
- Embroidery floss for flowers: yellow, brown/black, gold, cream, bright blue, yellow-green

cutting instructions

STEP 1 * From the light gray print, cut nine squares (9") for each base.

STEP 2 * From each of the floral fabrics, cut one strip (2½" x 45") for the block sashing.

STEP 3 * From the sashing/border fabric, cut nine strips (3" x 45").

STEP 4 * From the binding fabric, cut four strips (2½" x 45").

STEP 5 * Using the patterns from the pattern insert, and the Double Appliqué method on pages 8 and 9, trace, stitch, trim seam allowance, and complete the pieces for each of the nine flowers: sunflower, tulip, poppy, rose, tiger lily, iris, lobelia, poinsettia and pansy.

block assembly – make 9

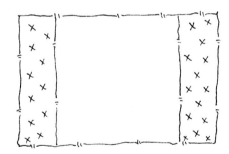

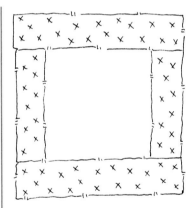

STEP 1 * With right sides together, sew a sashing strip to one side of a 9" square. Trim and press toward the sashing strip. Repeat for the opposite side of the block.

STEP 2 * Repeat Step 1 for the top and bottom edges of the block.

Sunflower

Tulip

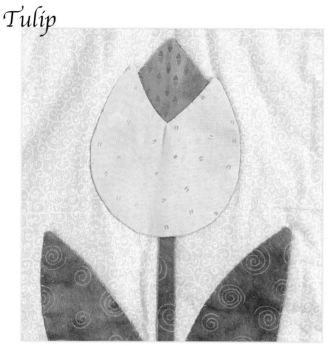

Refer to the stitch instructions on pages 19-25 for the embroidery of all flower blocks.

- The example shown is made with peach and watermelon colors, but you can use anything you like.
- Create the stem by using the Celtic method on page 11. Cut a 1" x 4½" piece of the green fabric, fold it in half, and sew with a ⅛" seam allowance.
- Stitch the bloom over the raw end of the stem, with the main flower overlapping the tip in the center.

- Use scraps of gold and medium brown fabrics.
- Make French knots with brown/black embroidery floss (one strand, wrapped four times).

Poppy

- Place the four large, orange petals in the center of the square, with the pointed ends touching.
- Stitch the smaller petals on top of the orange petals, slightly overlapping the edges of the larger petals.
- Use one strand of yellow embroidery floss to make French knots in the center of the flower. Wrap the needle three times. Cover an area a little smaller than a dime.
- Use black thread to stitch black eyelash yarn or other novelty fuzzy fibers around the center French knots.

Rose

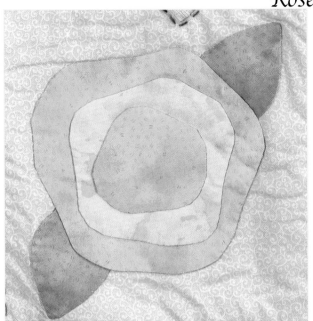

- Use scraps of light pink, medium pink and mint green fabrics.

Tiger Lily

- The tiger lily shown is made with medium orange print fabric, and embroidery floss in yellow-green and dark brown/black.
- Use three strands of the yellow-green floss to stem stitch the stamens.
- Stitch the end of the stamen with the dark brown/black floss, using one strand. Make two satin stitches for each end.

Iris

- Use scraps of white, purple and dark green fabrics.

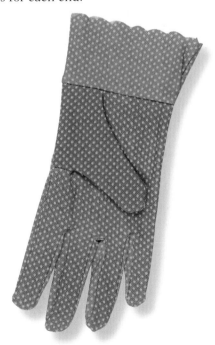

Lobelia

- The buds are appliquéd in a medium blue marble fabric.
- Use one strand of cream floss to make a V-shape using four satin stitches at the base of the flower.
- Use one strand of bright blue floss to make two lazy daisy stitches below the satin stitches.
- Use one strand of gold floss (wrapped three times) to make a French knot at the intersection of the satin and daisy stitches.
- Lightly draw stems for the lobelia blossoms with a pencil. Using two threads of the light lime green floss, stem stitch the stems.

Poinsettia

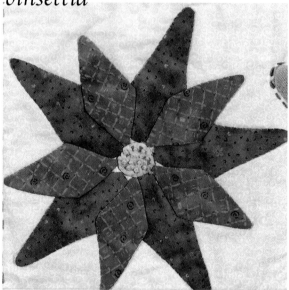

- Use scraps of red/rust, red/dark pink, and light lime green fabrics.
- Make about 12 French knots (one strand, wrapped four times) with gold embroidery floss in the center of the flower.

Pansy

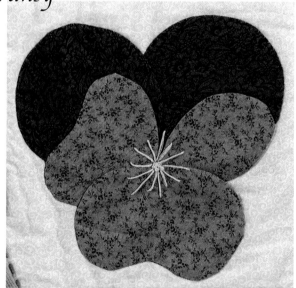

- Create the petals in various shades of purple.
- Use yellow floss (two strands) to create the straight lines radiating from the center of the flower.
- Make four to five French knots (one strand, wrapped three times) in the center of the flower.

quilt top piecing

STEP 1 * Arrange the nine flower blocks, three across and three down. Coordinate colors so they enhance each other best.

STEP 2 * Sew the sashing/border strips end to end, and press the seams open.

STEP 3 * Sew the sashing to the blocks along the vertical edges. Press the seam allowance toward the sashing.

STEP 4 * Sew the horizontal sashing between the rows of blocks, and press the seam allowance toward the sashing.

STEP 5 * Use the same fabric for the outside borders of the quilt. Attach the side borders, press the seam allowances toward the borders, and then attach the top and bottom borders.

quilt assembly

STEP 1 * Prepare the quilt for quilting, as shown on pages 12 and 13.

STEP 2 * Stitch the gloves randomly to the quilt top.

STEP 3 * Use a running stitch and six strands of embroidery thread to outline each block along the inner gray square and outer floral sashing.

STEP 4 * Sew the binding strips end to end. Press the seams open, and attach to the quilt, referring to the instructions on pages 14 and 15.

This would make an excellent block-of-the-month project for a group!

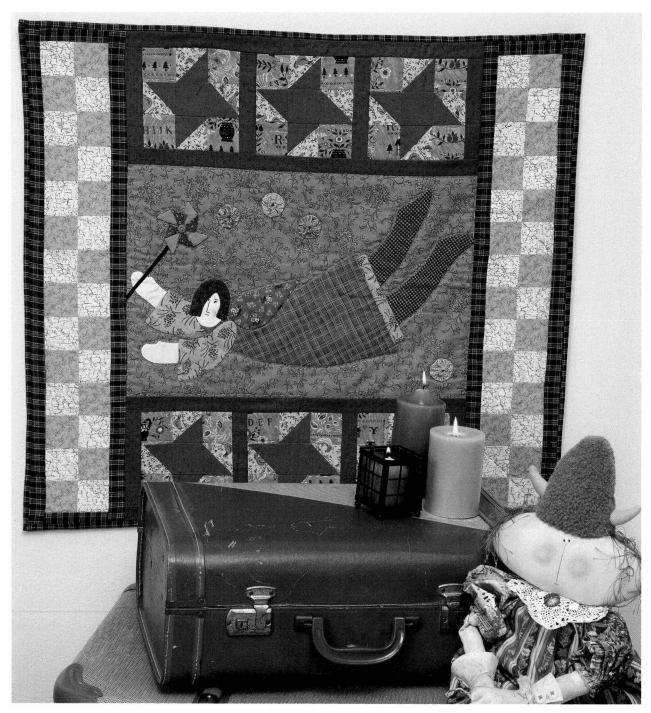

Finished Size: 33" x 29"

I Can Fly

As a child my favorite dreams were all about flying. In my dreams, I flew all over the farmyard, and the only frustration was when I began to sink to the ground. That was usually shortly before I woke up. I have, occasionally, as an adult, had very entertaining flying dreams. Flying seems almost a natural thing to do, doesn't it?

materials

½ yd. antique gold print fabric for appliqué base

Fat quarter of each of the following fabrics for blocks:
Tomato red print
Terra cotta print
Dark cream print
Taupe print
Cream print

¼ yd. purple print fabric for the sashing

⅝ yd. black plaid fabric for the borders and binding

Scraps of fabric:
tea-dyed muslin (face/hands)
dark brown print (hair)
black check (legs)
gold print (sleeves/dress)
lavender print (wing)
tomato red print (dress)
solid black (pinwheel handle)
rust and gold prints (yo-yos)
solid green (pinwheel)
green print (pinwheel)

1 yd. backing fabric

36" x 36" piece of thin cotton batting

Gold thread

Embroidery floss: dark brown, terra cotta and tan

Terra cotta button (½")

Acrylic paint: pink

cutting instructions

STEP 1 * From the antique gold print, cut one rectangle (24" x 16") for the appliqué base.

STEP 2 * From the tomato red print, cut six squares (2½") and 12 squares (2⅞"). Cut each of the larger squares in half diagonally, for a total of 24 triangles.

STEP 3 * From the terra cotta print, cut 24 squares (2½").

STEP 4 * From the dark cream print, cut 12 squares (2⅞"). Cut each in half diagonally, to make a total of 24 triangles.

STEP 5 * From both the taupe and the cream prints, cut two strips (2½" x 42") for the checkerboards.

STEP 6 * From the purple print, cut four sashing strips (1½" x 22") and eight sashing strips (1½" x 6½").

STEP 7 * From the black plaid, cut four binding strips (2½" x 42"), four sashing strips (1½" x 30½"), and four sashing strips (1½" x 4½").

STEP 8 * From both the green solid and the green print, cut two squares (3") for the pinwheel. Cut each in half diagonally, for a total of eight triangles.

STEP 9 * Using the patterns from the pattern insert, trace, stitch, trim seam allowance, and complete the flying woman pieces. Follow the directions for Double Appliqué on pages 8 and 9.

STEP 10 * Using the pattern from the pattern insert, cut out four circles from the rust and gold scraps for yo-yos.

flying woman

STEP 1 * Appliqué the flying woman to the antique gold rectangle, using the photograph as a guide.

STEP 2 * Refer to the stitch instructions on pages 19-25. Use one thread of dark brown floss to stem stitch the nose, mouth, upper eye line and eyebrow.

STEP 3 * Use one strand of dark brown floss to make a French knot for each eye. Wrap the needle four times.

STEP 4 * Dry-brush the cheek with the acrylic paint, per instructions on page 17.

STEP 5 * Trim the appliqué base to 22½" x 14½".

pinwheels

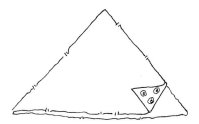

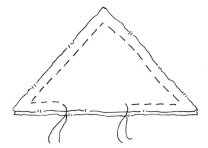

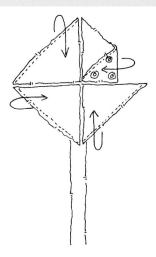

STEP 1 * To create the pinwheel, lay one solid green 3" triangle on a green print triangle with right sides together.

STEP 2 * Stitch around the triangle, leaving a 1" opening for turning.

STEP 3 * Turn right-side out and press.

STEP 4 * Repeat Steps 1-3 to create a total of four pinwheel units.

STEP 5 * Place the pinwheel units at the top of the appliquéd pinwheel stick so they form a square. Fold the right outer corner of each pinwheel unit toward the center, and tack it in place.

STEP 6 * Place the pinwheel in the flying woman's hand, and appliqué in place. Stitch a button to the center of the pinwheel.

yo-yos

Create the yo-yos, following the instructions on page 28. Arrange them in a pleasing manner and stitch down.

star blocks

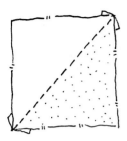

STEP 1 * Sew together one tomato red print triangle and one dark cream print triangle to make a square.

STEP 2 * Press the seam allowance toward the red triangle. The pieced square should be 2½" square. Repeat to make 24 squares.

STEP 3 * Lay out four triangle-squares. Add a tomato red print 2½" square in the center and four terra cotta print 2½" squares at each corner.

STEP 4 * Sew the squares together in rows. Press the seam allowances toward the red and terra cotta squares.

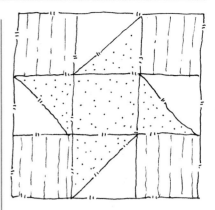

STEP 5 * Sew the rows together to make a star block. Trim the block, if necessary, to measure 6½" square. Repeat, to make a total of six star blocks.

quilt top piecing

STEP 1 * Refer to the diagram to lay three star blocks and four purple print sashing strips (1½" x 6½") in a row. Stitch them together. Press the seam allowances toward the sashing strips.

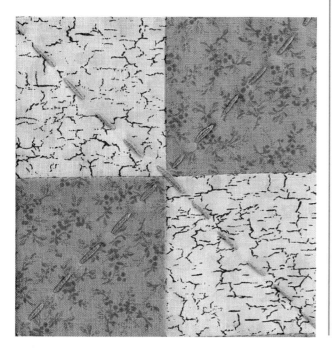

STEP 2 * Stitch a sashing strip to the top and bottom edges of the row (1½" x 22½"). Trim, if necessary, to measure 8½" x 22½". Repeat to make a second row of stars.

STEP 3 * To make the checkerboard rows, stitch one taupe print 2½" x 42" strip and one cream print (same size) to make a strip set. Press the seam allowance toward the taupe fabric. Repeat to make a second strip set.

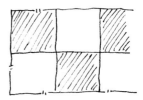

STEP 4 * Cut the strip sets into a total of 28 segments (2½").

STEP 5 * Sew the pieces together in a row, alternating the colors in checkerboard style. The completed strip should measure 4½" x 28½" (14 segments). Repeat to make a second checkerboard strip.

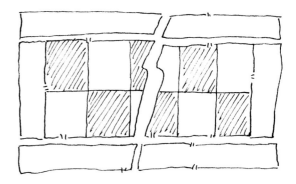

STEP 6 * Sew a 1½" x 4½" piece of black plaid sashing strip to each short end of the checkerboard strips. Add a 1½" x 30½" black plaid sashing strip to the top and bottom edges of the strips to make two checkerboard border units. Press the seam allowances toward the black strips. Trim the checkerboard units to measure 6½" x 30½", if necessary.

STEP 7 * Stitch a row of stars to the top and bottom edges of the appliquéd base. Press the seam allowances toward the base.

STEP 8 * Stitch one checkerboard row to each side edge of the base to complete the quilt top.

quilt assembly

STEP 1 * Assemble the quilt per the instructions on pages 12 and 13.

STEP 2 * Refer to the stitch instructions on page 21. Using coordinating embroidery floss, stitch a running stitch around each star, the flying woman and her block. Crisscross stitches through the checkerboard squares.

STEP 3 * Sew the binding strips together end to end, pressing the seam allowances open. Bind the quilt per directions on pages 14 and 15.

SUMMER

I used to think spring was my favorite
season, but when I am out on my hands and
knees in my garden, pulling weeds,
picking fresh vegetables and
flowers, or diligently building a
new fence, I think I'm in heaven.
Summer also means hanging
out my flag and being grateful to live
in a free land. It means taking walks in the
cool evening, bike rides and family picnics.
Summer is a great time of year!

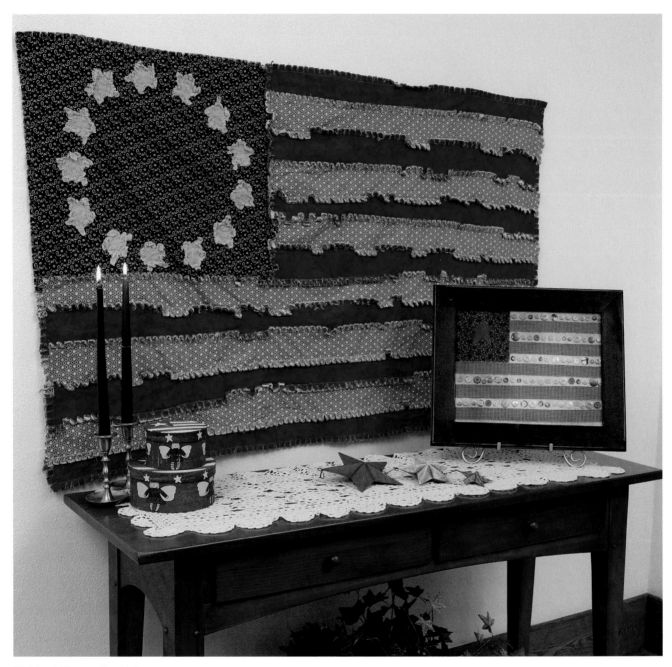

Finished Size: 54" x 33"

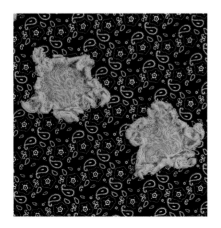

Raggy Flaggy

When my daughter, Vanessa, was 18, she made this wonderful little wall hanging for a newsletter article that I was writing. We liked the quilt so much, we both wanted it for ourselves, but we didn't have time to create another one. This book has provided the excuse for making another one. Here's Vanessa's "Raggy Flaggy."

materials

⅔ yd. each of two blue print fabrics for field
1¼ yd. each of two red print fabrics for stripes
1¼ yd. each of two cream/ecru print fabrics for stripes and stars
Matching thread

cutting and piecing instructions

Note: All seam allowances will be ½" for this project.

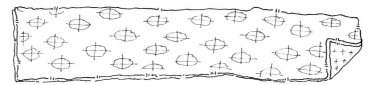

STEP 1 * Place the red fabrics wrong sides together, and cut four strips roughly 3¾" x 36". If they are a little out of proportion, that is just fine.

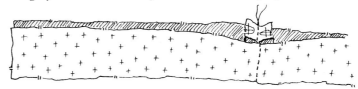

STEP 2 * Cut an additional four red strips approximately 3¾" x 45". Sew each color of strip end to end, pressing the seam open. Do not sew the 36" strips end to end.

STEP 3 * With the strips wrong sides together, cut them into three 60" lengths.

STEP 4 * Place the cream/ecru fabrics wrong sides together, and cut three strips ¾" x 36".

STEP 5 * Cut four strips 3¾" x 45", and sew end to end, as you did for the red.

STEP 6 * Cut the cream/ecru strips into 60" lengths.

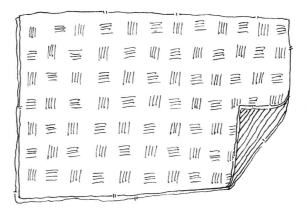

STEP 7 * Place the blue fabrics wrong sides together, and cut a rectangle which is roughly 20" x 24". The edges should be straight, but the rectangle doesn't have to be perfectly angled.

STEP 8 * Using the pattern from the pattern insert, cut 13 stars from two layers of white/ecru prints (right sides facing upward).

STEP 9 * Arrange the stars on the blue field, making sure they are at least 1" away from the raw edges.

STEP 10 * Stitch the stars to the field, ½" from their raw edges.

flag assembly

Note: *The raggy side will be referred to as the right side of fabric and the smooth side will be referred to as the wrong side.*

STEP 1 ✳ Select the fabrics that are to show as the front of the flag, and place a set of 36" red and a set of 36" white strips, right sides together.

STEP 2 ✳ Sew along the long edge through all four layers. Keep adding alternate colors until you have three stripes of each color.

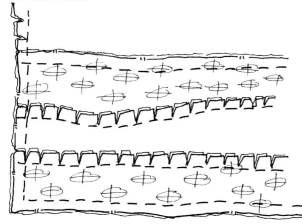

STEP 3 ✳ With right sides together (the right side having the seam allowances showing), stitch the first set of stripes to the two layers of blue field. The top stripe color should be red.

STEP 4 ✳ Trim the bottom stripe even with the blue field, if necessary.

STEP 5 ✳ Stitch the remaining 60" strips together as you did for the first six. Stitch them to the bottom of the blue field.

STEP 6 ✳ Machine stitch ½" from the outside edges of the flag.

STEP 7 ✳ Use sharp scissors to clip the seam allowances, including the stars, every ½". Throw the "flaggy" into the washing machine and dryer, and you will see how "raggy" your little patriotic creation will become!

Note: *If you wash and dry once more, it will look even more raggy.*

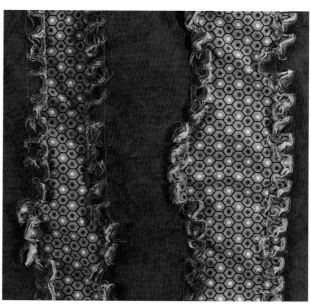

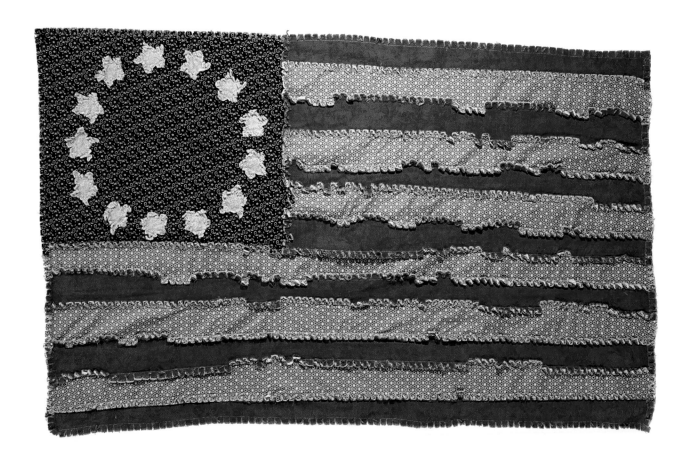

Finished Size: 12" x 24" (unframed)

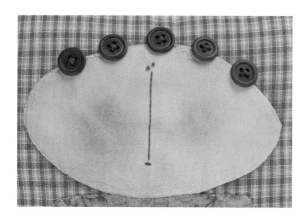

Miss Liberty

This flying Miss Liberty holds her little flag high above her head, showing her patriotic spirit. She is fashioned after a doll I designed that used a wood paddle as a base. You also can create a matching pillow.

materials

- ½ yd. ecru print fabric for background
- 3 fat quarters of coordinated patriotic print fabrics
- Fat quarter of tea-dyed fabric for face and hands
- 14" x 26" piece of thin cotton batting
- 5 ceramic star buttons (red, white, blue)
- Small flag (approx. 3½" x 5")
- Acrylic paint: burnt umber, red
- Embroidery floss: black, medium brown, red
- Quilting thread: Black or navy blue
- Frame or wooden shelf with 12" x 24" opening
- 12" x 24" piece of cardboard

instructions

Note: *This little quilt is framed by a wooden shelf/frame purchased from the craft store. I painted the frame with black acrylic paint, and when it was dry and lightly sanded, I added raw sienna acrylic paint, leaving some of the black peeking through. Spray with a matte sealer to finish.*

A piece of cardboard was cut to fit within the back of the frame (12" x 24"), and was covered with the thin cotton batting. The size of background for this project was 14" x 26". The quilt top was then pinned to the cardboard, leaving 1" margins on all sides. Bring the margins to the back of the cardboard, and glue in place.

As an option, you can add a backing and binding (see pages 12-15) to make a little wall hanging instead of a framed piece.

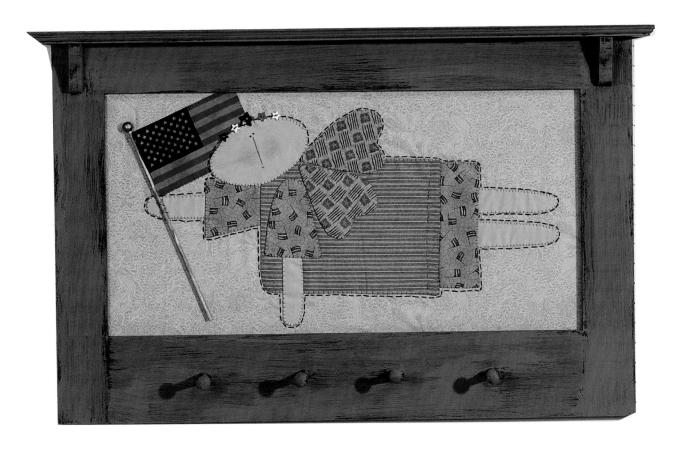

instructions

STEP 1 * Using the patterns from the pattern insert and the Double Appliqué method on pages 8 and 9, create the arms, legs and head from the tea-dyed fabric, and the clothing from the patriotic prints.

STEP 2 * Transfer the face per the instructions on page 10. Refer to the stitch instructions on pages 19-25. Use the medium brown floss (one strand) to stitch the nose using the stem stitch. The eyes are black French knots, with two threads, wrapped four times. The mouth is a single thread, stitched three or four times.

STEP 3 * Dry brush the cheeks with the red acrylic paint, following the instructions on page 17.

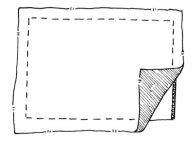

STEP 4 * Cut a piece of fabric to fit the cardboard, as designated above.

STEP 5 * The little flag was antiqued per instructions on page 18. You can antique the wood by this method, as well. Let it dry thoroughly.

STEP 6 * Use the quilting thread to stitch the lower skirt to the apron, and then center the entire design onto the fabric and pin in place.

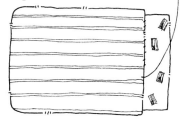

STEP 7 * Stitch the doll to the background, tucking one corner of the flag under her head, as pictured.

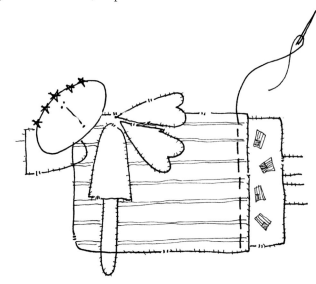

STEP 8 * Embellish the lower edge of the apron with the brown embroidery floss (two strands), making running stitches.

STEP 9 * Use the brown floss to stitch the ceramic star buttons on top of her head as a crown.

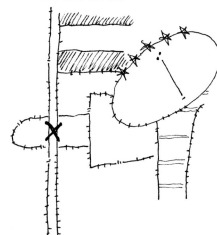

STEP 10 * Secure the wooden dowel (flag pole) to Miss Liberty's hand, by making X-shapes with the brown floss.

STEP 11 * Outline the doll's body and head by making running stitches with the black embroidery floss (two strands).

STEP 12 * Finish the quilt referring to the instructions on pages 12-15.

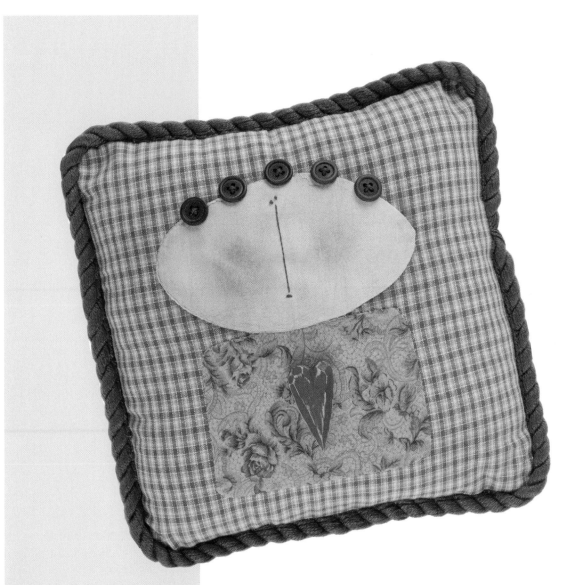

Miss Liberty Pillow

For a coordinating project, I put together a little pillow, which is a variation of the "Miss Liberty" quilt. I used the head pattern from Miss Liberty and created a torso by stitching a 3¼" x 4½" rectangle, with the corners rounded. The head and torso are appliquéd with the Double Appliqué method (pages 8 and 9), and the embroidery is the same as Miss Liberty. To create a hairdo, use five dark green buttons, stitched with red floss. A small wooden heart can be hot-glued to the front of her torso as an ornament. The pillow is made from two 10" squares, with 1⅓ yards of red cording and a little stuffing.

Finished Size: 11" x 14", unframed

Long May She Wave

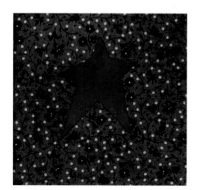

This wonderful little framed wall flag can be put together in an afternoon. I have very strong and proud feelings about our great nation, and I have begun to display flags as part of my home decorations. I was able to purchase a beautiful tea-dyed replica of Betsy Ross's flag, which hangs proudly in my hallway. When I was younger, some of my wonderful teachers taught us to memorize historical and patriotic works of literature, including the Preamble to the Constitution, The Gettysburg Address and part of Patrick Henry's speech. In the past few years, I have re-read some of the wonderful writings of people like Benjamin Franklin and George Washington. These were truly men worth emulating. May liberty continue to prevail.

materials

Scraps of fabric: blue and red prints

Fat quarter off-white, tea-dyed fabric print

13" x 16" piece of thin cotton batting

80 assorted off-white/tan buttons

Rusty star (approx. 4" tall)

11" x 14" frame

White fabric glue

Hot glue (optional)

11" x 14" matte board or cardboard

instructions

STEP 1 * Cut a rectangle (11" x 14") from the off-white background fabric. Leave ⅜" border all around the edges undecorated, to fit under the edges of the frame.

STEP 2 * Tear a 5¼" blue square. Glue it to the upper left corner. *Note: Apply as little glue as possible, but get it close to the edges.*

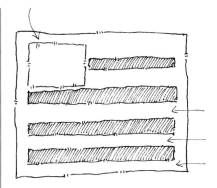

STEP 3 * Tear five strips of red (approximately 1" x 14"). Following the photo, lightly glue them in appropriate places. Leave about 1½" from the bottom stripe to the lower edge of the flag.

STEP 4 * Cut a piece of matte board or cardboard to fit inside the frame.

STEP 5 * Cut a piece of thin cotton batting to fit the cardboard.

STEP 6 * Apply glue to the edges of the cardboard, and adhere the batting to the cardboard.

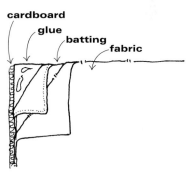

STEP 7 * Apply glue to the edges of the flag, and adhere the fabric to the batting.

STEP 8 * Place the flag inside the frame, and hot-glue buttons on each off-white stripe. Vary sizes and design as you go.

STEP 9 * Glue the rusty star to the center of the blue field.

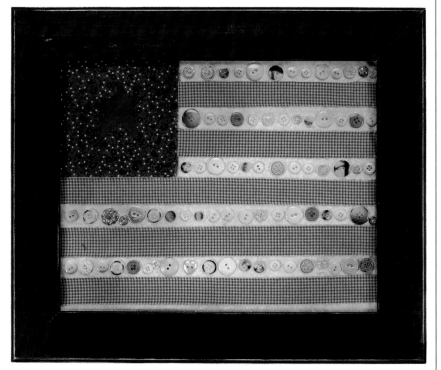

Finished Size: 11" x 14"

Shaker Proverb

Some of my favorite recipes come from the Shaker cookbooks that I have. The Shakers seem to have a knack for adding wonderful combinations of herbs to flavor their food. Imagine adding fennel to chicken soup!

Apples bring to mind homemade apple pie, apple crisp and applesauce.

materials

⅓ yd. taupe cotton flannel for the background
Scraps of fabric for the borders and apples
Scraps of brown and moss green wool felt for leaves and stems
11" x 14" piece of thin cotton batting
11" x 14" piece of cardboard
Frame with an 11" x 14" opening
Embroidery floss: terra cotta, pale olive green and black
13 dark blue buttons (⁵⁄₁₆")

cutting instructions

STEP 1 * From the taupe flannel, cut a rectangle (9½" x 12") for the background.

STEP 2 * From the border scraps, cut two strips (2" x 9½") and two strips (2" x 15").

STEP 3 * Using the leaf pattern from the pattern insert, cut 18 leaves from the moss green wool felt.

STEP 4 * Using the apple pattern from the pattern insert, trace, and cut three stems from the brown wool felt.

STEP 5 * Using the apple pattern from the pattern insert, trace, and stitch three apples, per the instructions for Double Appliqué on pages 8 and 9.

assembly

STEP 1 * Transfer the branch and lettering from the pattern insert to the background rectangle. See page 10 for instructions.

STEP 2 * Use two threads for all embroidery. Refer to the stitch instructions, pages 19-25.

STEP 3 * Embroider the branch lines with terra cotta floss, using a stem stitch.

STEP 4 * Use the stem stitch to embroider the lettering with pale olive green floss.

STEP 5 * Apply the apples to the background. Use matching thread color.

STEP 6 * Use the straight stitch to attach the leaves along the branch and on the apples. Attach the stems in the same manner.

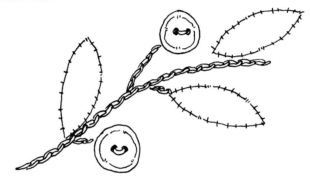

STEP 7 * Stitch the buttons in place along the branch.

STEP 8 * Attach the side borders (2" x 9½"), pressing toward the border. Repeat for the top and bottom borders (2" x 15").

STEP 9 * Cut a piece of cardboard to fit the frame opening.

STEP 10 * Glue a piece of batting to the cardboard, and then lightly glue the stitchery to the batting, trimming as needed.

STEP 11 * Place the piece in the frame, and secure it.

Finished Size: 18" x 29"

Shaker Apple Curtains

These apple curtains are the perfect accent for any kitchen.
You can easily fashion a table runner using the same method.

materials

2 purchased tea towels (18" x 29")
2 fat quarters of red fabric for the apples
2 coordinating fat quarters for the border and loops
Scraps of green wool felt
Embroidery floss: medium brown

cutting instructions

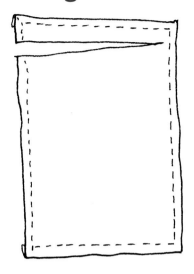

STEP 1 * Trim off the top edge of the tea towel (hemmed edge only). Leave the other edges intact.

STEP 2 * Measure the width of the tea towel. Cut two border strips for each towel, a total of four for this project. The strips should be 1" longer than the width of the towel and 3" wide. The towel shown is 18" wide, so the border strips measure 3" x 19".

STEP 3 * From the loop fabric, cut four 2" x 22" strips.

STEP 4 * Using the apple pattern from the pattern insert, trace, stitch, trim seam allowance and complete three apples for each tea towel, using the Double Appliqué method on pages 8 and 9. Make two apples from the plaid and one apple from the homespun solid for each towel.

STEP 5 * Using the leaf pattern from the pattern insert, trace, and cut out three leaves from the green wool felt.

loops and border

STEP 1 * Fold the loop strips in half, right sides together, and stitch ¼" from the long edges.

STEP 2 * Turn the loops right-side out and press them.

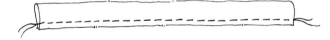

STEP 3 * Cut the loops into 6" lengths. You will need a total of 10 for the two curtains.

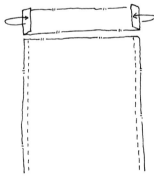

STEP 4 * Take each border strip and press the ends under so they are each the exact width of the tea towel (18").

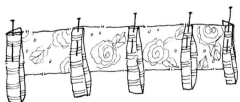

STEP 5 * Fold each loop in half, and pin the first loop flush to the left border strip edge. Pin to the right side of the fabric. Measure 4½" from the left edge, and pin the next loop, then pin the subsequent loops at 9" and 13½". The last loop is pinned flush to the right folded edge of the border.

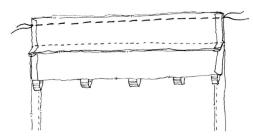

STEP 6 ✱ Place another border strip on top of the loops, matching raw edges, and stitch through all layers, leaving a ⅜" seam allowance. Press in half, with the wrong sides together.

STEP 7 ✱ Place one layer of the border on the cut edge of the tea towel. Right side of the fabric border on the wrong side of the tea towel. Stitch together. Press the seam allowance toward the border.

STEP 8 ✱ Press under the remaining edge of the border, and pin to the right side of the tea towel, covering the previous stitching.

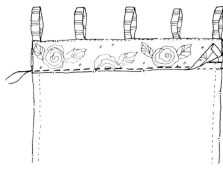

STEP 9 ✱ Topstitch the border to the tea towel.

apples

STEP 1 ✱ Center and pin the three prepared apples to the lower edge of the curtain, about 2" from the bottom. Stitch in place.

STEP 2 ✱ Stitch the leaves in place, just off center at the top of the apple.

STEP 3 ✱ Use two threads of the medium brown embroidery floss to stem stitch (see page 19), a stem in the middle of each apple. Let them curve slightly to the right or left as you stitch.

finishing

Place a rod in the loops, and the curtains are ready to welcome your family to supper.

Apple Valance

You easily can make a little apple valance to match
your curtains by purchasing an ivy garland (this one
has honeysuckle vine mixed in) from your craft store.
Tear 1" strips of the remaining fabric and, randomly
tie around the vine. Trim the ends to 3".

To attach the latex apples, poke a small hole in the
bottom of the apple with a very small awl. Fold an
8" length of 20-gauge craft wire in half, and twist it
together. Trim the ends so they are twisted, leaving no
wire to poke out at an angle. Apply a little hot glue to
the cut ends, and insert the wire into the apple. Apply
a little more hot glue to the wire; push it into the
garland firmly. Wrap the end around, if necessary, to
hold the apple in place. Tack little nails into the wood
window frame, and wire the garland in place, using
green floral wire.

Finished Size: 13" x 16½"

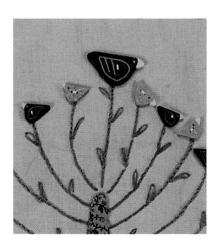

Shaker Tree of Life

For many years, I have been fascinated by the Shaker culture. As America's oldest religion, its history is replete with tales of persecution, success and demise. The beautiful edifices and furnishings built by the Shaker people still stand, restored and cared for, as monuments to industrious, good people. These little stitcheries are my own tribute to the Shakers and their influence on today's decorating.

materials

- ½ yd. wheat-colored fabric for the background
- ⅛ yd. tan/white gingham fabric for border No. 1
- ⅛ yd. dark green stripe fabric for border No. 2
- ⅛ yd. medium green print fabric for border No. 3
- ½ yd. backing fabric
- Scrap of brown print fabric for tree trunk
- 14" x 18" piece of thin cotton batting
- Embroidery floss: moss green, pale moss green, moon yellow, dark wheat
- 17 decorative buttons (use ½" hearts, birds, fruit or whatever you like)

cutting instructions

STEP 1 * Cut a rectangle (9½" x 13") from the wheat-colored fabric for the background.

STEP 2 * From the tan/white check, cut two strips (1½" x 45") for border No. 1.

STEP 3 * From the green stripe, cut two strips (1½" x 45") for border No. 2.

STEP 4 * From the medium green, cut two strips (1" x 45") for border No. 3.

STEP 5 * Cut a rectangle (14" x 18") for the backing. This will be trimmed later.

tree

All embroidery uses two threads. Refer to the stitch instructions on pages 19-25.

STEP 1 * Transfer the image of branches and letters to the background fabric. See page 10 for instructions.

STEP 2 * Create the tree trunk from the scrap of brown print and the pattern found on page 89. Use the Double Appliqué method described on pages 8 and 9.

STEP 3 * Embroider the branches and letters using the stem stitch.

STEP 4 * Create the leaves by stitching a single lazy daisy stitch.

STEP 5 * Use the moss green for leaves and branches and the pale moss green for lettering. Use the dark wheat floss to make small running stitches next to lettering, as indicated on pattern.

quilt top assembly

STEP 1 ✱ With right sides together, stitch border No. 1 to each side of quilt top. Press the seam allowances toward border. Attach the top and bottom borders to the quilt.

STEP 2 ✱ Repeat this sequence for border No. 2 and border No. 3.

STEP 3 ✱ Place the quilt top on the batting, and trim the batting to fit the top.

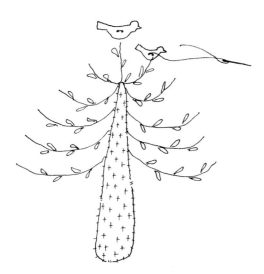

STEP 4 ✱ Stitch the buttons to the tree, one at the end of each branch.

STEP 5 ✱ Trim the backing to fit the quilt top. Place right sides together, on top of the quilt top.

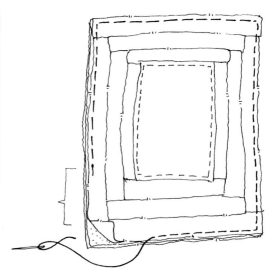

STEP 6 ✱ Stitch around the edges of the quilt, leaving a 3" opening on one side.

STEP 7 ✱ Turn the quilt right-side out. Press on the back side, making sure to press out the edges close to the stitching.

STEP 8 ✱ Refer to the stitch instructions on page 22. Whipstitch the opening closed.

STEP 9 ✱ Use a running stitch to quilt around each of the borders. Use moon yellow floss next to border No. 3, pale moss floss next to border No. 2, and dark wheat floss next to border No. 1.

Trunk
(stitch one
on doubled
fabric)

Shaker Tree of Life Words

AUTUMN

There is something wonderful and melancholy about the approach of autumn. Leaves begin to turn vivid colors, the air takes on a crisp quality, and the days are noticeably shorter. The unmistakable signs of winter begin to show — in fact, an occasional bit of snow may fly, and all the sweaters and jackets come out of the drawers. Halloween is a great deal of fun, and then it's time to reflect on the Pilgrims and our wonderful Thanksgiving holiday. Time to put that extra quilt on the bed!

Finished Size: 36" x 36"

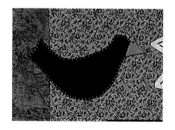

Old Crow Farm

I lived on the Old Crow Farm until I left for college. It was a place of warmth and love, filled with exceptional memories.

the old crow farm

There is quite a bit to say about The Old Crow Farm, as it was the place
I spent my childhood. Each of the motifs on the quilt has a story related
to my little heaven on earth. When I was little, I
remember grown-ups asking me where
I lived. I described the place as
being close to the highway, two
miles south of Romeo, Colo.
Many times, they would respond, "So you
live at the old Crow place?" My dad explained that
the family who built the house had the last name of
Crow. I lived on the Old Crow Farm until I left for college. It
was a place of warmth and love, filled with exceptional memories.

My siblings and I all dressed up for Sunday school.

One of the blocks has a small red building, pictured with an open door. That is the pump house. My father spent so much time in there fixing the pump that he said he figured if he was sent to hell, he would be assigned to fix pumps there.

There were crows that lived near our farm. My mother showed me a nest, up very high in one of our old cottonwood trees. I remember thinking that crow's nests were very large, and very messy looking, built with rather large twigs.

The second row has two buildings. The red building with a galvanized tin roof was the granary. My father stored grain, which he used to entice the milk cows into the barn when it was milking time. The granary attic was accessed by a large heavy staircase, which was lowered out of the ceiling. There were several wonderful antique picture frames stored there, and one of them belongs to me now. One of

the not-so-pleasant aspects of playing in the granary was that I learned that when you roll around in the grain, it makes you itch.

The green and white house was our old farmhouse. My sister and I slept in the upstairs gabled room, which was on the right side of the house. The room was painted a very pale blue, and my mother made ruffled curtains from white chintz fabric with pale blue polka dots. I thought it was heavenly.

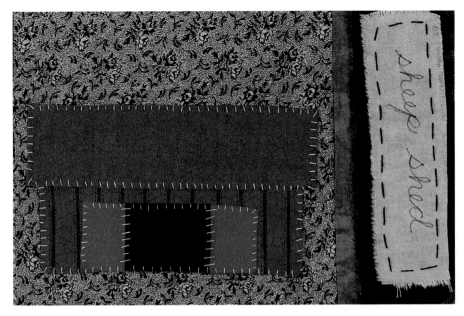

The third row features a sunflower, sheep and the sheep barn. Sunflowers and dandelions were my favorite flowers, and I picked them and decorated our little green wagon so we could have little parades in our yard.

Summer was a glorious time for flowers, and the pastures often had beautiful wild iris in bloom, too.

Now, contrary to the ideas you might have about sheep, they are not the placid, sweet-natured animals you might think. They are real troublemakers, as any farmer knows. My siblings and I often were asked to help "drive" the sheep from one area to another. We would start down a road or trail, and things would be fine for about five minutes. Inevitably, one of these sweet creatures would take it into her head to investigate the tiny opening in the fence, and decided that it might actually be where we wanted her to go. As one sheep would wriggle her way into the forbidden territory, all the rest leaped and jumped after her. It was like the whole bunch had gone crazy. I learned the best swear words while driving sheep. Eventually the sheep would be rounded up, and once a year we would go through the process of shearing sheep. The victims were herded into the giant sheep barn to wait their turn. I soon learned several important things: Sheep don't smell very good in enclosed buildings; sheep are very homely without their wool; when you jump into the large burlap bag to help compact the wool, you have to be examined later for sheep ticks; and you smell like a sheep until you get in the bath.

Row four has the famous pump house and a single little innocent chick. Once a year, we ordered baby chicks, and they arrived in large cardboard boxes with little round holes, about the size of a nickel. They were sweet and beautiful and so very soft when they first came to us. Soon, however, they reached adolescence, and the soft yellow stuff disappeared, replaced by spiked white feathers. Does this sound familiar? The adolescent nature also began to appear, and some of the chickens began to pick on each other. Not a pretty sight. Soon enough, however, they were just the right size to make into delicious fried chicken, and the rest were put in the freezer for yummy dinners for the rest of the year.

The bottom row features the little beehives, the quonset and milk barn, and finally the chicken coop. The beehives were kept a mile away from the house, and the bees had vast fields of yellow clover from which they produced their beautiful, light honey. Mr. Hansen actually owned the bees, but as payment for letting them stay on our land, he brought us a 5-gallon tin of honey each year. We all loved honey on my mother's homemade bread.

The quonset was used for storing tractors and other interesting equipment, and it was once a residence for a few turkeys. We never raised them again, as their temperament was nasty and belligerent. We did eat them, though. Attached to

names, which I won't mention out of common decency.

Finally, the chicken coop was a place of great fear for me. When I was very young, my mother found a nest that a hen made in a stack of tires in the shop. She let my sister and I each hold one of the tiny chicks, then put them away before she returned to the house.

My sister and I decided we wanted to hold the chicks again, so I climbed up to retrieve them. The mother hen apparently felt threatened by that, so as soon as I went outside, she flew up at me, knocked me down and pecked at me while flailing me with her wings. I screamed for help, and my mother came out to rescue me. My sister also was screaming, and to this day, we both have fairly intense chicken (and all feathered friends) phobia. You can imagine the horrors of being assigned to gather up the eggs in the chicken coop.

As you make the quilt, you can certainly adapt the pieces or create new ones that reflect your own story.

the quonset was our milk barn, which consisted of stanchions, which helped hold the cows in place while they ate their ground-up grain during the milking. We had several milk cows, the most famous of which were Blackie and Tiny. Both were Black Angus cows, and they were excellent milk cows. Blackie was placid and sweet. Tiny wasn't. She wasn't above swatting you with her tail or kicking the milk over, if you didn't watch her. Tiny had several other

My sister and me nearby the infamous chicken coop.

The plentiful sunflowers adorned our little green wagon.

materials

- ⅓ yd. black/tan print fabric for blocks
- ¼ yd. black/tan plaid fabric for four-patch blocks
- ¼ yd. black print fabric for four-patch blocks
- ½ yd. green solid fabric for borders
- 1¼ yd. backing fabric
- ⅓ yd. black print fabric for binding fabric
- Scraps of wool felt and various printed fabrics for the appliqué motifs
- 38" x 38" piece of thin cotton batting
- Embroidery floss: yellow/orange, black, medium green, dark brown, dark gray
- Cream-colored quilting thread
- 4 buttons (¼")

cutting instructions

STEP 1 * From the black/tan print fabric, cut 13 squares (6½") for the alternate blocks.

STEP 2 * From the black/tan plaid fabric, cut 24 squares (3½") for the four-patch blocks.

STEP 3 * From the black print fabric, cut 24 rectangles (3½" x 2") and 24 squares (2") for the four-patch blocks.

STEP 4 * From the brown print fabric, cut 24 squares (2") for the four-patch blocks.

STEP 5 * From the medium green fabric, cut four border strips (4" x 45").

STEP 6 * Tear 1½" strips of tea-dyed fabric and 2" strips of black fabric for the labels.

STEP 7 * Using the patterns from the pattern insert, trace, stitch, trim seam allowance, and complete the buildings and animals, using the Double Appliqué method on pages 8 and 9. The appliqué details are described below.

appliqués

The appliqué details all are made from wool felt. Refer to the stitch instructions on pages 19-25 for all embroidery stitches. Use a straight stitch to apply all the felt pieces to the fabric motifs with cream quilting thread.

STEP 1 * Crow: Cut a gold felt beak and stitch to the bird.

STEP 2 * Banner: Stem stitch the banner with two threads of dark brown for the letters and a medium green running stitch ¼" from the edge of the banner.

STEP 3 * Granary: Use dark gray felt for the roof, black for the upper window and light gray for the door and shuttered windows.

STEP 4 * Farmhouse: Apply a green roof, porch roof, pillars and door. The chimneys are brick red, and the windows are black.

STEP 5 * Sunflower: Use light gold felt for the petals, medium green for the stem and brown fabric for the center.

STEP 6 * Sheep: The ear, face and legs are black felt. The body is ivory felt.

STEP 7 * Sheep barn: The roof is dark gray, the open doors are rust, and the doorway is black.

STEP 8 * Pump house: Apply a black door opening and a gray roof to the fabric building and door.

STEP 9 * Chick: Cut a gold felt beak and stitch to the bird. The eye is a French knot with two threads wrapped four times, and the legs are stem stitched using two threads of yellow/orange floss.

STEP 10 * Beehives: All the hives have black doors. The right one is trimmed with gold felt. The right and left hives each have a brown felt post. The bees are light gold with black stem-stitched stripes (one thread), French knot heads (two threads, wrapped four times) and cream felt wings.

STEP 11 * Quonset: Stem stitch an upside-down U-shape on one end with dark gray floss (one thread). The window uses pale green, and the door is medium gray with two buttons for embellishment at the top.

STEP 12 * Milk barn: This barn is attached to the open end of the quonset and has a medium green roof, green door (two buttons on top) and a black window.

STEP 13 * Chicken coop: Use rust for the door, black for the windows and light gray for the roof.

four-patch blocks

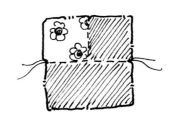

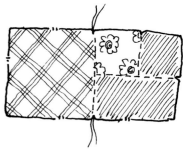

STEP 1 * Sew each brown 2" square to a black 2" square. Press the seam allowance toward the brown fabric.

STEP 2 * Sew each 3½" x 2" rectangle to the two squares, arranging them so the brown square is on the upper right corner. Press the seam allowance toward brown fabric.

STEP 3 * Sew one of the pieced squares from Step 2 to a black/tan plaid block so the brown square is touching the plaid square. Repeat for all 24 sets.

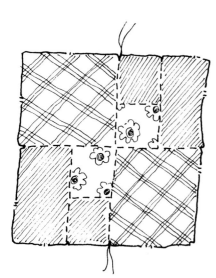

STEP 4 * Sew the sets together so each four square has the brown squares "kissing" each other in the center. Press the seams open.

STEP 5 * Sew five rows of five blocks, alternating the pieced blocks and the 6½" black/tan print blocks.

quilt top assembly

STEP 1 * Whipstitch the motifs to the rows of squares as pictured. *Note: The crows will have to be stitched last, as they overlap the green border.*

STEP 2 * Sew the rows together. Match the corners, and press the seams open.

STEP 3 * Sew a 4" green border strip to the top and bottom edges of the quilt. Press the seam allowances toward the border.

STEP 4 * Repeat for the side borders, trimming the ends square.

appliqué labels

STEP 1 * Use a fabric stabilizer to stiffen the fabric torn for the appliqué labels, following the directions on the can. Stiffening the fabric makes it easier to write on.

STEP 2 * Use a permanent brown felt-tip pen to write the labels, and place each label on a piece of the torn black strip.

STEP 3 * Use two threads of black floss to stitch the label to the quilt.

finishing

STEP 1 * Embellish the quilt top with additional buttons, if you like.

STEP 2 * Assemble and bind the quilt following the instructions on pages 12-15.

STEP 3 * Quilt as desired. The example was machine stippled over the entire quilt top, avoiding the appliqués and labels.

Finished Size: 17" x 17"

Horse Pillow

One of my great, unrealized dreams was to ride horses on a regular basis. I was only able to ride very occasionally; my father's family owned horses when he was a boy. They were the old-fashioned, workhorses fitted with harnesses and other equipment meant to pull thrashing machines, plows and other working implements. I remember seeing a few old-timers who still preferred the workhorse to the tractor. Leonard Nielson was one of my favorite old farmers. He had all of his teeth missing and refused to wear dentures, but he could still enjoy a wonderful steaming hot steak —and he always used his horse to take care of farming chores. This horse pillow is dedicated to Leonard and others of a vanishing breed.

materials

- ½ yd. black upholstery-weight brocade for appliqué base
- Fat quarter of each of the following fabrics:
  - Taupe flannel for horse
  - Gold print for inner border
  - Black/white check for outer border
  - Olive print for braid trim
  - Rust print for braid trim
  - Taupe print for braid trim
- ½ yd. backing fabric
- Scraps of wool felt: gold, rust, black, brown, and taupe for horse harness
- Scraps of black/white plaid fabric for corner triangles
- 2 yd. black/taupe cotton cord edging
- Embroidery floss: olive green
- 16" pillow form

cutting instructions

STEP 1 * Using the pattern from the pattern insert and the taupe flannel, trace, stitch, trim seam allowance, and complete the horse, using the Double Appliqué method on pages 8 and 9.

STEP 2 * Using the patterns from the pattern insert, trace and cut out the harness pieces from the felt scraps.

STEP 3 * From the black upholstery weight brocade, cut one square (12½") for the appliqué base.

STEP 4 * From the black and white plaid, cut four squares (2⅞").

STEP 5 * From the gold print, cut two strips (1¼" x 12½") and two strips (1¼" x 14") for the inner border.

STEP 6 * From the black and white check, cut two strips (2" x 14") and two strips (2" x 17") for the outer border.

STEP 7 * From each of the olive, rust, and taupe prints, tear five strips (1" x 22").

braid trim

STEP 1 * Sew each color of the torn strips end to end, pressing the seams open. You will have three separate sets of strips.

STEP 2 * Tie the strips together, in a knot, and braid the strips together. *Note: It is easier to braid the strips if you roll each color of strip into a fabric ball and use a safety pin to hold the ball from unraveling. As you braid, you can unpin about 18" at a time and braid until all of the fabric is used.*

pillow top

STEP 1 * Appliqué the horse to the black upholstery-weight brocade base, centering it.

STEP 2 * Use contrasting quilting thread to stitch the harness to the horse. Add appropriate embellishments if desired.

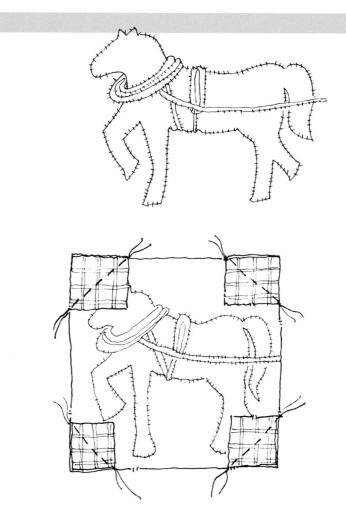

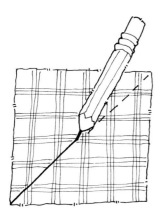

STEP 3 * Use a pencil to draw a diagonal line through each black and white plaid square.

STEP 4 * Pin the square to each corner of the black wool, with the penciled line at a 45-degree angle to the lower edge of the base.

STEP 5 * Stitch along the marked lines, and trim the seam allowance to ¼". Press the seams open.

borders

STEP 1 * Use the gold print for the inner border. Sew the 1¼" x 12½" strips to the top and bottom edges of the pillow center. Press the seam allowances toward the border. Repeat for the side edges, using the 1¼" x 14" strips.

STEP 2 * Attach a black and white check 2" x 14" border strip to the top and bottom edges of the pillow center. Press the seam allowance toward the border. Repeat for the side edges of the pillow, using the 2" x 17" strips.

STEP 3 * Pin the braid to the outside of the gold print border. Sew the braid to the pillow top, overlapping the ends and tucking the raw edges underneath.

STEP 4 * Stitch a feather stitch (see page 21) over the top of the seam that is between the black wool base and its borders.

finishing

STEP 1 * Pin the black/taupe cord edging to the pillow top, with the flat edge of the cording along the raw edges. Follow the instructions for cording on page 16.

STEP 2 * With right sides together, sew the backing to the pillow top, leaving a large opening for inserting the pillow form. Turn the pillow right side out, insert the pillow form, and whipstitch the opening closed.

Finished Size: 26½" x 26½"

The Queen of the Harvest

Fall always was a wonderful time, as that was the time the harvest moon was so big and bright. Apples were in season, and it was time to get a costume ready for the Halloween party at school. At school, we played in huge piles of leaves and enjoyed the wonderful glimpses of summer days, which grew colder and frostier at night.

The Queen of the Harvest, with her corn scepter, rules the autumn festivities and you easily can create all the harvest accessories, including the corn made from felt and buttons and "planted" in bales of straw, which you can find in the craft store. Make several pumpkins, and find a corner in which you can display your own fruits of the harvest.

materials

- ⅝ yd. medium green fabric for background
- ¼ yd. black swirl print fabric for sleeves and dress
- ¼ yd. orange print fabric for blocks
- Fat quarter of each of the following:
  - Black print fabric with olives or circles—anything to resemble eyeballs for four-patch blocks
  - Fall print fabric for dress
  - Wool felt: light peach for head, hands, and legs
- Scraps of felt: dark green, medium green, brown, plum and tan for corn scepter and pumpkins
- Scraps of coordinating fabrics for pumpkins
- 1 yd. backing
- ¼ yd. dark green print fabric for binding
- 30" x 30" piece of thin cotton batting
- Embroidery floss: medium yellow and light purple
- Embellishment yarns, such as eyelash yarn
- Quilting thread: black and tan
- Acrylic paint: red for cheeks

cutting instructions

STEP 1 ✳ Using the patterns from the pattern insert, trace, stitch, trim seam allowance and complete the pumpkins, arms, dress and apron, using the Double Appliqué method described on pages 8 and 9.

STEP 2 ✳ Using the wool felt, cut out the head, hands, legs, corn scepter, shoes, one pumpkin, stems and leaf.

STEP 3 ✳ From the medium green print, cut a square (18½").

STEP 4 ✳ From the black olive print, cut 20 squares (2").

STEP 5 ✳ From the black print, cut three strips (2" x 45").

STEP 6 ✳ From the orange print, cut four strips (2" x 45").

STEP 7 ✳ From the binding fabric, cut three strips (2" x 45").

log cabin blocks

Make 20 basic blocks.

STEP 1 ✳ Sew the three black print strips end to end. Press the seams open.

STEP 2 ✳ Sew the four orange strips (2" x 45") end to end. Press the seams open.

STEP 3 ✳ Place the center square (2") on the end of the black strip, right sides together, and place on the sewing machine.

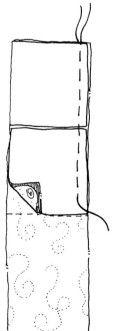

STEP 4 ✳ Sew the first block, place the next square close to the first square, and continue sewing until all 20 blocks are stitched along the strip.

STEP 5 ✳ Cut the blocks apart, using a ruler to ensure the strips and squares are straight.

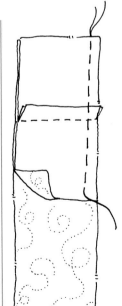

STEP 6 ✳ Press the seam allowance toward the center block for all seams.

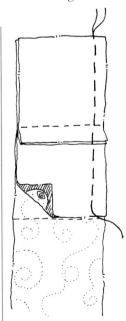

STEP 7 ✳ Place the block/strip piece, right sides together, on the black strip. Stitch all 20 pieces, as you did before.

STEP 8 ✳ Repeat this step for the orange print. **Note:** *The blocks are stitched, consecutively, in a counter-clockwise direction.*

background assembly

STEP 1 * Sew two sets of four blocks for the vertical sides and two sets of six blocks for horizontal sides. Be sure to have the blocks facing the same way, with the orange on the upper and left-hand sides of each block.

STEP 2 * With right sides together, sew one set of four blocks to the top of the green fabric square (18½"), and the other set to the bottom edge. Press toward the green fabric. Repeat for the top and bottom edges of the quilt.

appliqués

STEP 1 * Refer to the stitch instructions for all embroidery on pages 19-25. Embroider the face, using two threads of dark brown floss for the nose and a French knot for each eye, wrapping the needle four times. Dry brush the cheeks with red paint (see page 17).

STEP 2 * Stitch the ear of corn onto the dark green felt. Add the husks, stitching them onto the felt. Cut around the outside of the ear of corn, leaving ⅛" border of dark green felt.

STEP 3 * Referring to the photo for placement, layer and pin the queen, her scepter and the pumpkins to the background.

STEP 4 * Use quilting thread to stitch the pieces to the background. Use a color of quilting thread that contrasts with the appliqué piece.

STEP 5 * After you stitch the scepter in place, use two 1" lengths of angora or other wispy yarn to create the corn floss. Stitch the center of the yarn to the top of the ear of corn.

STEP 6 * Embroider the corn with yellow floss, making French knots with one full strand of floss. Wrap the needle three times.

STEP 7 * Use the purple floss (two threads) to make three laces on top of the shoe, and attach the sole with the floss, using running stitches.

STEP 8 * Use the dark brown floss (two threads) to make a running stitch vine on the top of each pumpkin.

STEP 9 * Use the white/multicolor eyelash yarn to make a hairdo. Cut two lengths of yarn, 1½" long, tied with a knot at the center, and stitch to the center top of head.

finishing

STEP 1 * Assemble the quilt, batting and backing as indicated on pages 12 and 13.

STEP 2 * Sew the three binding strips together end to end. Attach the binding a scant ½" from the edge of the quilt. Finish the binding per instructions on pages 14 and 15.

Finished size: 7½" (ear)

Harvest Gatherings

Stitch several pumpkins using various orange fabrics to make a collection for your mantle—hang the carrots on pegs in the room if you like, and make a corn patch in the corner of your entry to greet holiday guests. You can even use a carrot to glue a name card to, as a novel place setting decoration for each guest.

corn

materials

- 10" square light gold felt for each ear
- Fat quarter green fabric for husks
- Embroidery floss: medium gold
- Bale of straw (medium size)
- Novelty yarn for corn silk
- Approx. 30 assorted yellow buttons (no shanks)
- Stuffing
- 3/8" wooden dowel 24" long for each ear
- Acrylic paint: medium green
- Hot glue gun/sticks
- White craft glue
- Very-fine grit sanding pad
- Spray sealer (matte)

cutting instructions

STEP 1 * Using the pattern from the pattern insert, trace, and cut out two pieces of gold felt for each ear of corn.

STEP 2 * From the green fabric, tear two or three 1½" strips of fabric for the husks.

STEP 3 * Cut the dowels in different heights.

stalk assembly

STEP 1 * Paint each dowel medium green, and sand lightly. Spray with a matte sealer.

STEP 2 * Use sharp scissors or a craft knife to make a slit in the bottom of each ear of corn.

STEP 3 * Push the dowel into the corn to make a "hole" in the batting. The dowel should poke into the corn 3" to 4". Remove the dowel, insert glue into the hole, then re-enter the dowel, making sure it is inserted straight. Let the glue dry.

ear assembly

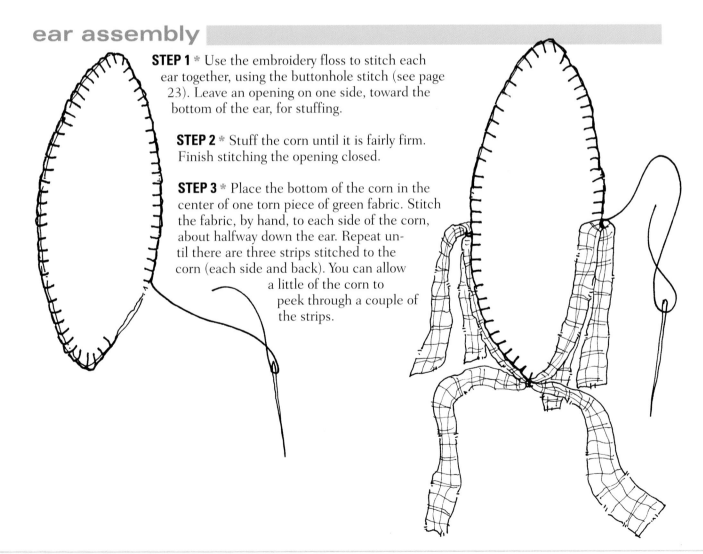

STEP 1 * Use the embroidery floss to stitch each ear together, using the buttonhole stitch (see page 23). Leave an opening on one side, toward the bottom of the ear, for stuffing.

STEP 2 * Stuff the corn until it is fairly firm. Finish stitching the opening closed.

STEP 3 * Place the bottom of the corn in the center of one torn piece of green fabric. Stitch the fabric, by hand, to each side of the corn, about halfway down the ear. Repeat until there are three strips stitched to the corn (each side and back). You can allow a little of the corn to peek through a couple of the strips.

finishing

STEP 1 * Tie extra fabric strips to the dowel to look like leaves. Leave the ends 5" to 6" long.

STEP 2 * Make a tassel from the yarn (see page 28). The tassel should go down the sides of the corn about 2".

STEP 3 * Use the hot glue to apply the buttons all over the ear of corn.

pumpkin

materials

- ⅓ yd. orange fabric
- Felt: green and brown
- Stuffing
- Embroidery floss: dark green, burnt orange
- Black craft wire
- White craft glue

Finished Size: 7" tall

cutting instructions

STEP 1 * Using the pattern from the pattern insert, trace, and cut four pumpkin pieces.

STEP 2 * Using the pattern from the pattern insert, trace, and cut a leaf shape from the green felt.

STEP 3 * Cut a piece of brown felt 2½" x 3½" for the stem.

vine, leaf, and twig assembly

STEP 1 * Cut about 15" of black craft wire, twist the end around a pencil, then use your hand to make swirls and loops in the wire. Leave about 4" of the opposite end straight. Make sure you wash your hands, as this wire really makes your hands dirty.

STEP 2 * Take the leaf, and using green floss, make a running stitch (see page 21) down the center of the leaf. Add further veins, if desired.

STEP 3 * Roll brown felt into a coil 2½" tall with a diameter of ½". Glue or stitch together to hold shape.

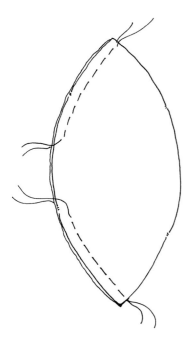

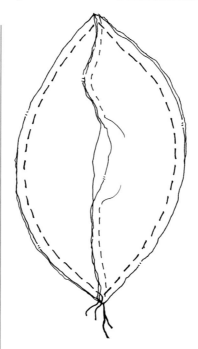

STEP 3 * Sew around the entire pumpkin, and turn right side out through the opening.

STEP 4 * Stuff the pumpkin firmly, and stitch the opening closed.

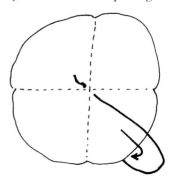

STEP 1 * Place two pumpkin pieces, right sides together, and sew, leaving a 4" opening for turning. (You will not have to leave an opening in the remainder of the seams.

STEP 2 * Sew the two remaining pieces together, and pin them to the first set, matching raw edges.

STEP 5 * Thread a needle with orange floss, and tie a knot at one end. Make a stitch at the bottom of the pumpkin (either end), where the seams intersect, and bring the thread around to the top of the pumpkin, in between the seam lines.

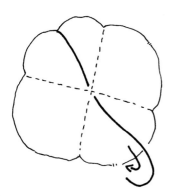

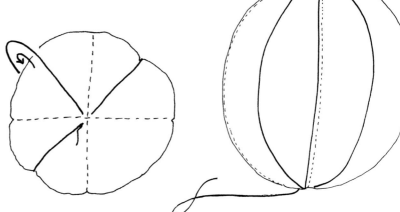

STEP 6 * Take a stitch at the top, then continue around the other side of the pumpkin, back to the starting point. Pull the floss slightly to indent the fabric.

STEP 7 * Continue this process until all the areas between the seams are sculpted, and then follow the seamlines as well. Tie a knot at the bottom of the pumpkin.

STEP 8 * Glue the stem to the top of the pumpkin.

STEP 9 * Add glue to the tip of the wire before insertion. Insert the wire vine into the pumpkin, next to the stem.

STEP 10 * Glue the leaf to the top of the pumpkin.

carrots

materials

Scraps of orange and green fabrics

Stuffing

Finished Sizes: 9" (large), 7" (small)

cutting instructions

STEP 1 * Using the pattern from the pattern insert, trace and cut out either a large or small carrot. (Only one piece is needed for each carrot.)

STEP 2 * Tear a strip of green fabric 1" to 1½" wide x 10".

carrot assembly

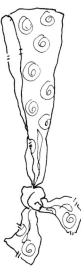

STEP 1 * With right sides together, sew the sides of the carrot together, leaving an opening at the top.

STEP 2 * Starting with a very small piece, stuff the stuffing into the tip of the carrot. Continue adding more stuffing until the carrot is firm. Do not stuff the top 1" of the carrot.

STEP 3 * Use a needle and strong thread to stitch a running stitch around the top edge of the carrot. Pull the stitches tight to gather, tucking raw edges inside. Make a knot.

STEP 4 * Fold the green strip of fabric in half. Make a knot about 4" from the fold.

STEP 5 * Trim off the ends to leave about 1" from the knot, then hand stitch the knot to the top of the carrot. You can use the green loop to hang the carrots on a peg shelf or just add to the other collection of vegetables on the harvest table.

Finished Size: 29½" x 29½"

Hi, Honey—I'm Home!

Unlike the worker bees, hardworking humans are not confined to one gender. Some of the most pleasant moments in my life were associated with work, both with my father and mother. I remember spring cleaning when my mother emptied out the cupboards, washed all the dishes and the inside of the cupboard, then put everything back again. We always asked about each of the special dishes, and heard the same answers every year while we helped put things away. When I went outside with my father to assist him with chores, such as distributing hay to the cows when the snow covered their pasture, we talked about his childhood. When we were finished and came back into the house, Mama fixed us a late supper of huevos rancheros and her homemade cocoa. "Hi Honey—I'm Home!" is all about that kind of warmth and affability. Home can be a happy place when people appreciate each other and remember to do little things for each other.

materials

1½ yd. blue fabric for background and backing
¼ yd. blue floral fabric for the border
⅓ yd. green plaid fabric for the four-patch blocks
⅓ yd. tan print fabric for the four-patch blocks
¼ yd. pink fabric for the binding
Scraps of yellow fabric for the bee
Scraps of felt: black, cream, red, rust, pink, gold and dark brown for bee, hive and heart
36" x 36" piece of thin cotton batting
Embroidery floss: rose pink, medium brown, black, gold, light green and red
Quilting thread: cream
4 unpainted wooden buttons (⅞" wide)
Acrylic paint: avocado green
Matte spray sealer

cutting instructions

STEP 1 * Using the patterns from the pattern insert and the yellow fabric, trace, stitch, trim seam allowance and complete the bee body using the Double Appliqué method described on pages 8 and 9.

STEP 2 * Using the patterns from the pattern insert and the appropriate colored felt, trace, and cut the wings (cream), the stripes (black), the head (black), the arms and legs (dark brown), the hands and feet (rust), the small heart (red), the large heart (pink), the beehive (gold), and the hole (dark brown).

STEP 3 * From the blue fabric, cut a 15½" square for the background.

STEP 4 * Using the green plaid, cut four 3" x 45" strips for the checkerboard border.

STEP 5 * Using the tan print, cut four 3" x 45" strips for the checkerboard border.

STEP 6 * From the border fabric, cut two strips (3" x 15½") and two strips (3" x 20½").

STEP 7 * From the pink fabric, cut three 2½" x 45" strips for the binding.

center panel assembly

STEP 1 * Refer to the stitch instructions on pages 19-25 for all embroidery. Stitch the stripes to the bee body, using the cream quilting thread and a straight stitch.

STEP 2 * Stitch the face with one thread of medium brown for the nose and two threads for the French-knot eyes (wrap four times). The mouth is stitched with two threads of rose pink, with a French knot wrapped four times.

STEP 3 * Stitch the body to the background with contrasting threads. Use one thread of black floss to stitch the wings and hive in place. Use cream thread for the arms, legs, head, heart and body.

STEP 4 * Stem stitch the antennae with one strand of black floss.

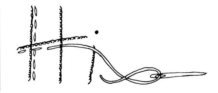

STEP 5 * The letters are stitched with two threads of gold floss, using the stem stitch. Add shadows to each part of the letters (right sides, undersides) using two strands of the red floss.

STEP 6 * The heart is attached with one thread of gold floss and a straight stitch.

inner border

STEP 1 * Sew a border to the top and bottom of the background fabric, pressing toward the borders (3" x 15½").

STEP 2 * Attach the side borders and press toward the borders (3" x 20½").

outer border

STEP 1 * Sew one green plaid strip to one tan print strip. Repeat for all four strips. Press the seams toward the green plaid.

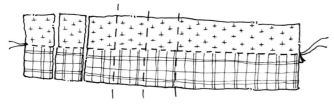

STEP 2 * Segment cut the strips into thirty 3" sections.

STEP 3 * Alternating the placement to create a checkerboard pattern, sew two sets of eight strips together for the top and bottom borders. The top left block should be the green plaid.

STEP 4 * Sew two sets of 12 segments together for the side borders. The upper left-hand block should be the tan print.

STEP 5 * Sew the top and bottom borders, comprised of 16 blocks to the background. Match the seams of the blue borders to the checkerboard borders. Press the seam allowances toward the checkerboard borders.

STEP 6 * Sew the side borders, comprised of 24 blocks, in place. Match seams. Press the seam allowances toward the checkerboard borders.

finishing

STEP 1 * Sew the binding strips end to end.

STEP 2 * Layer, bind and quilt the quilt. The example was machine stippled (see page 29) everywhere except over the appliqués.

STEP 3 * Use the red floss to make a running stitch (see page 21) around the outside edge of the blue background.

STEP 4 * Paint the buttons medium avocado green, sand the edges lightly, and spray with matte sealer. Stitch the buttons to the quilt with light green floss. Tie in a square knot on top of the button, and trim the ends to about ⅛".

Finished Size: 7½" x 10½"

Bee Skep

I remember the summer my brother was stung by some of the honeybees on our farm. He was out plowing, and I suppose he must have infuriated the bees by plowing up the alfalfa blossoms. At any rate, my brother was highly allergic to the bee stings, so I jumped in my father's old Ford pickup and drove him to the doctor for shots. I had no license, as I was underage, but that didn't matter to the bees or anyone else. That incident didn't deter us from enjoying the honey from those bees, or our fascination with the organization of a beehive. Just recently, I read a wonderful book, "The Secret Life of Bees," by Sue Monk Kidd. It's a book I plan to give to my daughter, my mother and my friends Robin and Darlene. The book is delicious! It makes me want to bake my favorite muffins and make a batch of honey butter to slather on top!

I'm not sure where the word bee skep comes from—perhaps a colloquial way of saying "bees keep," but it is really a beehive. A special thank-you to my friend, Sylvia, whose incredible floral style was the inspiration for the embellishments on this bee skep.

materials

1¾ yd. wheat-color cotton print fabric
24 feet acrylic rope, ½" diameter
Pip berries or other floral berries
2 silk hydrangeas, 1 pink, 1 purple (dried look)
3 silk sunflowers (dried look)
1 blue button thistle (dried look)
3 to 5 wooden bees, unpainted
Acrylic paint: black, cream and gold
Gel stain (brown)
Matte spray sealer
10" to 12" black craft wire (22-gauge) per bee
Hot glue gun and glue stick
3" large plastic craft needle

forming the hive

STEP 1 * Tear the fabric into 1½" strips.

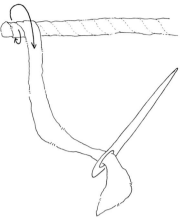

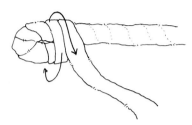

STEP 2 * Thread one strip of fabric into the eye of the craft needle. Wrap the opposite end of the fabric around the rope, overlapping the fabric so the rope doesn't show through.

STEP 3 * When about 4" or so of the rope is covered, twist the rope into a tight U-shape, and wrap the fabric around both sides of the U. Wrapping around both pieces forms a "bridge."

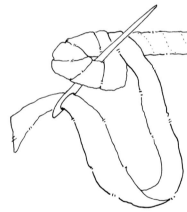

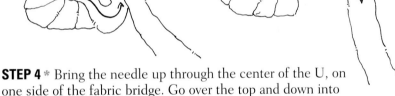

STEP 4 * Bring the needle up through the center of the U, on one side of the fabric bridge. Go over the top and down into the center on the opposite side of the fabric bridge.

STEP 5 * Wrap the rope three or four times, then fasten the loose end to the coil.
Note: *Always wrap the* **rope** *in a counter-clockwise motion.*

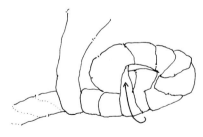

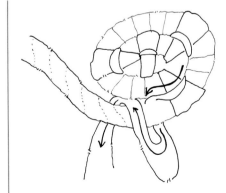

STEP 6 * After the rope is wrapped three or four times, insert the needle into the coil so the fabric covers two sections of the rope and makes a new bridge.

STEP 7 * Bring the needle up through the middle of the two ropes, then on the left side, over the top of the fabric bridge, and then down on the right, exiting at the bottom.

STEP 8 * Bring the fabric to the outside edge of the rope, and continue wrapping the loose rope and then fastening it to the coil. Repeat this sequence until the bee skep is complete.

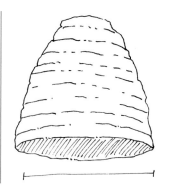

STEP 9 * You will form a very small, flat circle at the top, gradually forming a cone shape as you work. The base of the cone is approximately 7½" wide, and the height of the cone is about 10½".

STEP 10 * To finish, fasten the end of the rope so it gradually works inside the cone, then hand stitch the end of the fabric strip in place.

making the bees

STEP 1 * Paint the entire bee with the gold paint. Let it dry.

STEP 2 * Paint the head and stripes black.

STEP 3 * Paint the wings cream.

STEP 4 * After all the paint is completely dry, lightly sand the edges, and brush the gel stain onto the bee.

STEP 5 * Wipe the excess gel stain with a paper towel, and let the bee dry.

STEP 6 * Spray the bees with sealer.

STEP 7 * Drill a tiny hole in one of the bees to fit the craft wire.

STEP 8 * Cut a 10½" piece of wire, bend and curl it, then insert into the bee. Put a little bit of glue on the end. Set aside.

decorating the bee skep

STEP 1 * Use wire cutters to cut pieces of the pip berries. Place a little hot glue onto the end of the berry branch, and then insert it into the bee skep between the ropes.

STEP 2 * Glue the hydrangeas here and there, as single blossoms.

STEP 3 * Trim the sunflower stem to 2". Insert into the top of the hive, and glue in place.

STEP 4 * Trim the leaves from the remaining flowers and glue them underneath the base of the bee skep.

STEP 5 * Insert the wired bee into the top of the bee skep, and glue in place. Glue the other bees onto the bee skep.

WINTER

Although winter is not my favorite season, Christmas is my favorite holiday. I decorate much more lavishly for Christmas, and I love all the extra little lights that make the cold winter nights sparkle. The wonderful traditions that are part of winter include baking gingerbread cookies for friends and neighbors, selecting just the right gifts for the people I love, decorating trees at home and at the store, cuddling underneath a warm, flannel quilt, walking outside while the snow is falling, and reading a book by a warm fire. See, winter isn't so bad!

Finished Size: 20" x 22"

The Warmth of Home

This little wall hanging depicts the real meaning of any holiday season for me. The traditional symbol of welcome is the pineapple, and my whole philosophy of decorating a home revolves around creating an environment that is warm and inviting. Good food, the wonderful aromas of cooking, big overstuffed chairs and good lighting around a dining room table all are important elements of creating an ambience of welcome. Surrounding oneself with loved ones is the most important aspect of any holiday season, and this little creation is one of my ways of extending welcome.

materials

Fat quarter of each of the following fabrics:
Dark red flannel for background
Solid gold flannel for pineapple
Tan flannel for border
Scraps of green plaid flannel, purple print and tan plaid fabrics and green wool felt
26" x 28" piece of thin cotton batting
Embroidery floss: brick red, antique gold
Green button (1")
Tracing paper (white)
Quilting thread: red

cutting instructions

STEP 1 * From the dark red fabric, cut a rectangle (16½" x 18") for the background.

STEP 2 * Using the patterns from the pattern insert and the appropriate fabrics, trace, stitch, trim seam allowance and complete the pineapple (gold flannel), leaves (green plaid flannel), and large curved teardrops (purple print), using the Double Appliqué method described on pages 8 and 9.

STEP 3 * Using the pattern from the pattern insert and the green wool, trace, and cut out two smaller teardrop shapes.

STEP 4 * From the tan flannel, cut two border strips (2½" x 16½") and two border strips (2½" x 18").

STEP 5 * From the tan plaid, cut four squares (2½") for the cornerstones.

quilt top assembly

STEP 1 * Appliqué the pineapple, leaves and large purple teardrops to the background as shown.

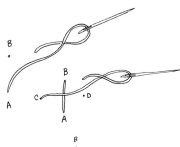

STEP 2 * Embroider the pineapple using two strands of antique gold floss. Stitch a series of small upright cross-stitches: Bring your needle up at A, go down at B, then bring your needle up at C, crossing over the first stitch and exiting down at D.

STEP 3 * Refer to the stitch instructions on pages 19-25 for all embroidery. Stitch French knots in between the crosses.

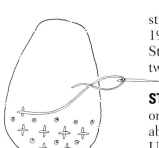

STEP 4 * Trace the lettering onto the fabric, centering above the pineapple leaves. Use two threads of gold floss to stem stitch the lettering.

STEP 5 * Using two strands of the antique gold floss and a straight stitch, attach the two small green felt teardrop shapes. One is stitched to the top of the right purple teardrop and the other is below the pineapple, in the center.

STEP 6 * Whipstitch the green wool felt teardrops to one of the fabric teardrops, and at the center below both teardrops.

borders

STEP 1 * Sew the border strips (2½" x 18") to the sides of the background and press toward the border.

STEP 2 * Sew one tan plaid square (2½") to each end of the remaining border strips (2½" x 16½"). Sew these strips to the top and bottom edges of the quilt top.

STEP 3 * Make running stitches around the outside edge of the red background, using the brick red (two threads) embroidery floss. Add more running stitches around the pineapple, leaves and large teardrops.

STEP 4 * Stitch the button to the left-hand purple teardrop using the antique gold floss.

STEP 5 * Have the quilt framed professionally, or add a backing and binding (see pages 12-15) to create a wall quilt.

The Snowman

Building a snowman is
one of the wonderful childhood
games we used to play at home
and school. At home, we used to
go to the back of the granary to
get coal pieces for the eyes and
mouth. Our mother grew a huge
garden, and we put straw bales
over the carrots so they wouldn't
freeze in the ground. When we
wanted fresh carrots, we just
pulled a bale away and dug them
up. They made great carrot cake
and a great snowman nose!

Finished Size: 14½" x 34"

materials

Scraps of the following fabrics for snowman:
  Celery print (A)
  Yellow/green print (B)
  Tea-dyed fabric (C)
  White-on-white print (D)
  Antique white print (E)
  Tan/white print (F)
  Ecru print (G)
  Light tan print (H)
  Tan print (I)
  Black print (J)
  Black/gray print (K)
  Black moiré (L)
  Cream/tomato print (M)
  Tomato print (N)
  Dark green print (O)
  Dark tan print (P)

1 yd. backing

⅛ yd. yellow/green print fabric for border

¼ yd. red fabric for binding

Wool felt: terra cotta, tomato red, white

Yarn: green chenille, yellow bouclé

20" x 40" piece of thin cotton batting

6 wooden buttons, painted black (½")

White plastic snowflake

Embroidery floss: dark brown, red

Acrylic paint: rosy pink

cutting instructions

STEP 1 * Cut fabric C into four squares (3") and fabric L into one square (3").

STEP 2 * Cut the following fabrics into the indicated number of 2" x 45" strips:

  Fabric A (3)
  Fabric B (2)
  Fabric D (1)
  Fabric E (1)
  Fabric F (1)
  Fabric G (1)
  Fabric H (1)
  Fabric I (1)
  Fabric J (1)
  Fabric K (1)
  Fabric M (10)
  Fabric P (1)

STEP 3 * Using the patterns on pages 130 and 131 and the appropriate fabrics, trace, stitch, trim seam allowance and complete the mittens (Fabric N) and scarf (Fabric O) per the Double Appliqué instructions on pages 8 and 9.

STEP 4 * Using the patterns on page 130 and the appropriate wool felt, cut out two small mittens (white), two small hearts (red), and a nose (terra cotta).

snowman body assembly

STEP 1 * Assemble four log cabin blocks per the diagrams:

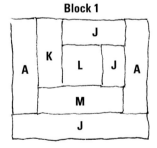

Block 1

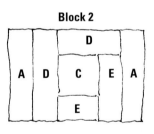

Block 2

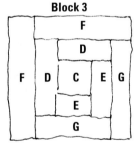

Block 3

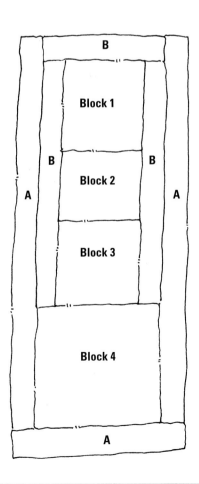

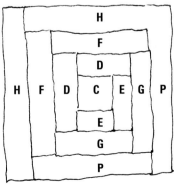

Block 4

STEP 2 * With right sides together, stitch the four blocks together in a row, following the diagram above and right.

STEP 3 * Sew Fabric B to the sides and the top of the three top log cabin blocks.

STEP 4 * Sew block No. 4 (see diagram) to the bottom of the blocks.

STEP 5 * Sew Fabric A to the sides and the bottom of the blocks.

embellishments

STEP 1 * Stitch the small white mittens and red hearts to the red appliqué mittens.

STEP 2 * Couch the green chenille yarn on the white mittens using red embroidery floss. Couch the yellow bouclé yarn on the green scarf using matching thread.

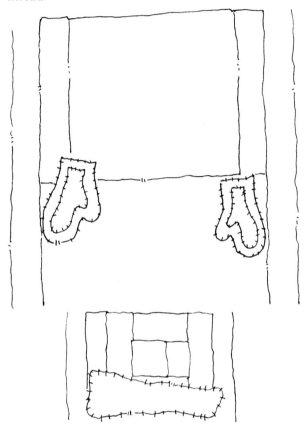

STEP 3 * Stitch the mittens and scarf in place, noting the diagram for the approximate placing.

STEP 4 * Refer to the stitch instructions on pages 19-25. Use the dark brown floss (two threads) to stem stitch the strings for the mittens.

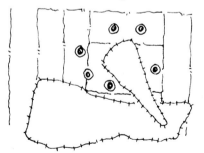

STEP 5 * Stitch the nose onto the face at an angle, using straight stitches.

STEP 6 * Dry brush the cheeks rosy pink (see page 17).

STEP 7 * Noting the photo for placement, attach the buttons for the eyes and mouth.

finishing

STEP 1 * Assemble and bind the quilt per instructions on pages 12-15. The binding is 2½" wide.

STEP 2 * Quilt as desired. The example shown was stippled over the snowman body and borders. The hat, scarf, mittens and nose were left alone.

STEP 3 * Using the red embroidery floss, (two threads) stitch a running stitch around the perimeter of blocks 2, 3 and 4.

STEP 4 * Tie a 2" wide strip of fabric N into a knot, and trim off each end to 1½". Stitch to the lower right side of the hatband.

STEP 5 * Stitch a snowflake to the upper left corner of the quilt.

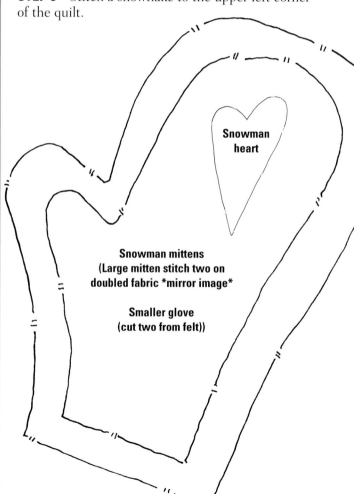

Snowman heart

Snowman mittens
(Large mitten stitch two on doubled fabric *mirror image*

Smaller glove
(cut two from felt))

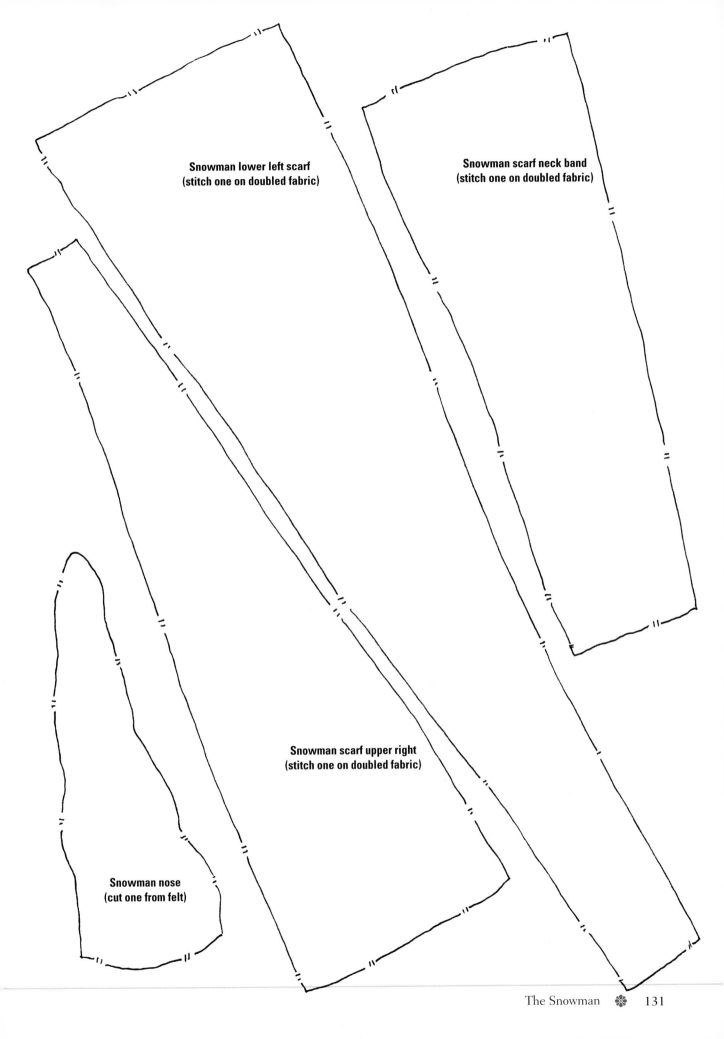

Snowman lower left scarf
(stitch one on doubled fabric)

Snowman scarf neck band
(stitch one on doubled fabric)

Snowman scarf upper right
(stitch one on doubled fabric)

Snowman nose
(cut one from felt)

Finished Size: 35½" x 36½"

The Peacemakers

I work part-time as a display designer at a retail craft store. I count everyone there as one of my friends, but I am especially close to two friends Sylvia and Olivia. Sylvia is a fellow designer and she amazes me with her energy and ability to work "outside the box," especially with her floral designs.

One of my other close friends is Olivia. Olivia has a great sense of humor, and she always has a smile. She has a passion for quilting, as well as a degree in civil engineering. Her grandmother was a medicine woman for the Navajo tribe in Arizona, where Olivia spent part of her childhood. Sylvia, Olivia and I have a deep and everlasting friendship. I often think that if we lived 200 years earlier, we might have had more difficulty in establishing such a friendship. How glad I am that things have changed and that we all have a chance to work together and share our love of creativity.

materials

- 1 yd. background fabric
- ⅓ yd. navy print for borders
- Fat quarters of the following:
  - Blouse fabric No. 1
  - Blouse fabric No. 2
  - Skirt fabric No. 1
  - Skirt fabric No. 2
  - Dress fabric
  - Tea-dyed fabric for faces and hands
  - Medium taupe for faces and hands
  - **Note:** You may want two different shades to represent various skin colors
- Scrap fabric for corner stones, aprons and ties
- 1 yd. backing fabric
- ⅓ yd. navy print binding fabric
- Scraps of felt for boots, legs and star
- 40" x 41" piece of thin cotton batting
- Assorted buttons, beads, feathers, printed twill tapes, trims for embellishment
- Scraps of eyelash yarn, other funky yarns for hair
- Embroidery floss: black, medium brown, terra cotta and wine
- Quilting thread: terra cotta
- Acrylic paint: terra cotta

cutting instructions

STEP 1 * From the background fabric, cut a rectangle (32½" wide x 31½" tall).

STEP 2 * Using the patterns from the pattern insert and the appropriate fabrics, trace, stitch, trim seam allowance, and complete the heads, hands, legs and articles of clothing, following the instructions for Double Appliqué on pages 8 and 9.

STEP 3 * From the scraps of wool felt, trace, and cut out the boots, moccasins and the star.

STEP 4 * From scraps of a tan print, cut four squares (3") for each corner.

STEP 5 * Cut two border strips (3" x 32½") and two border strips (3" x 31½").

STEP 6 * Cut four strips (2½" x 45") of the binding fabric.

face embellishment

STEP 1 * Refer to the stitch instructions on pages 19-25 for all the embroidery. Stem stitch the nose with a single thread of the medium brown floss.

STEP 2 * Make French knots (two threads), wrapped four times for the eyes.

STEP 3 * The mouth is a single thread of terra cotta floss, stitched three to four times.

STEP 4 * The cheeks are drybrushed with the terra cotta paint, using the method described on page 17.

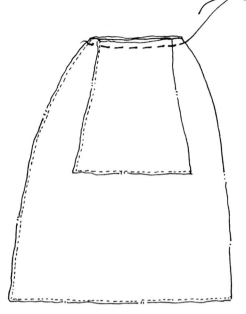

STEP 1 * Using the quilting thread and a straight stitch, appliqué the aprons to the two skirts belonging to the outside dolls.

STEP 2 * Center, layer, and pin the bodies, remaining clothing and star on the background fabric. Appliqué them in place using the quilting thread and a straight stitch.

STEP 3 * Using the photo as a guide, add the yarn for the hair. Stitch with the quilting thread.

STEP 4 * Embellish the clothing, as you like. I stitched pre-printed pieces of twill tape to the bottom of each doll to serve as inspirational labels.

Note: *You can find little goodies like this in scrapbook sections of the craft stores.*

borders

STEP 1 * Sew two border strips (3" x 32½") to the top and bottom edges of the quilt. Press the seam allowance toward the border.

STEP 2 * Sew a 3" tan print block to each end of the remaining border strips (3" x 31½"). Press the seam allowance toward the border.

STEP 3 * With right sides together, sew the side borders in place, matching the seams at the corners. Press the seam allowances toward the borders.

finishing

STEP 1 * Sew the binding strips end to end.

STEP 2 * Assemble and bind the quilt per the instructions on pages 12-15.

STEP 3 * Quilt as desired. The quilt shown was machine quilted using the stippling method (see page 29) throughout the background area.

STEP 4 * Using the wine-colored floss, (two threads) make a running stitch around the outside edge of the background, about ¼" from the border fabric.

Finished Size: 25" x 37"

And a Partridge in a Pear Tree

This song has been one of the Christmas songs we probably all learned in grade school because it was a great tool for memorization. At some point, it started to make about as much sense as "99 Bottles of Beer on the Wall," but we all still sang the song.

Last Christmas Day night, as our family got together to celebrate my birthday (yes, Christmas really is my birthday), my son, Clint, retrieved something from his room, which he read to us. It changed my viewpoint of "The Twelve Days of Christmas" in a major way. Without going into too much detail, it was a historical account of how this song came to be. Apparently, due to religious persecution, some of the Roman Catholics who lived in the British Isles needed a method to teach their children their Catechism without getting in trouble with the local authorities. This song was developed to teach some of the basic principles, the main example being that the partridge in the pear tree was a direct reference to Jesus on the cross. I thought that was so interesting that it made me want to make a quilt as a unique way to celebrate the holiday of Christmas and pay tribute to those people who were truly devoted to freedom of religion.

materials

- 1¼ yd. rose print background fabric
- Fat quarter red print fabric for flowerpot and yo-yos
- Fat quarter red/green print fabric for flowerpot and yo-yos
- Scraps of dark brown print and medium green print fabrics for tree
- Scraps of pale blue, yellow and lavender fabrics for hearts
- Wool felt:
- Small scraps of olive green
- 6" x 8" dark gray/blue
- 6" x 12" rust
- 9" x 12" antique gold
- 1¼ yd. backing fabric
- ¼ yd. medium brown print fabric for binding
- 31" x 45" piece of thin cotton batting
- Embroidery floss: medium green, dark brown, red
- Quilting thread: navy blue
- 6 red buttons (⅝")

cutting instructions

STEP 1 * Using the patterns from the pattern insert and the appropriate fabrics, trace, stitch, trim seam allowance, and complete two hearts and the flowerpot using the Double Appliqué method described on pages 8 and 9.

STEP 2 * Using the patterns from the pattern insert and the appropriate colored felt, trace, and cut out the following: six pears (gold), four pears (rust), six leaves (olive green), and a partridge (gray/blue).

STEP 3 * From the medium green fabric, tear strips for the branches in each of the given lengths, 1½" x 10", 1¼" x 16½", and 1½" x 20½".

STEP 4 * From the dark brown fabric, tear one strip (1¼" x 23") for the trunk.

STEP 5 * From the background fabric, cut a rectangle (25½" x 37½").

STEP 6 * Cut six 3½" circles for the yo-yos, four from the red print and two from the red/green print.

STEP 7 * From the binding fabric, cut three strips (2½" x 45").

tree assembly

STEP 1 * Pin the flower pot about 1½" from the lower edge of the background.

STEP 2 * Insert the trunk into the middle of the pot, so the top edge of the pot overlaps it about ¼".

STEP 3 * Refer to the stitch instructions on pages 19-25 for all embroidery. Use six strands of the dark brown floss to stitch the trunk in place with running stitches along the outside edges.

STEP 4 * Place the branches horizontally across the trunk. The lower branch should be 5" from the top edge of the pot, the center branch 12" from the top edge of the pot, and the top branch 19" from the top edge of the pot.

STEP 5 * Use six strands medium green floss to stitch the branches in place with running stitches.

STEP 6 * Appliqué the partridge to the top of the tree, covering the raw edges of the trunk top.

STEP 7 * Make six yo-yos (see page 28).

STEP 8 * Using the red floss, sew a button in the center of each yo-yo, and stitch the yo-yo to the ends of the branches.
Note: Stitch the red/green print yo-yos at the ends of the middle branch.

STEP 9 * Appliqué the six olive green leaves to the gold pears, using the navy blue thread.

STEP 10 * Place a gold pear under each end of the branches. Appliqué in place with the navy quilting thread and a straight stitch. Stitch the remaining four rust pears under the middle and lower branches.

STEP 11 * The hearts are layered and stitched to the upper right and left corners.

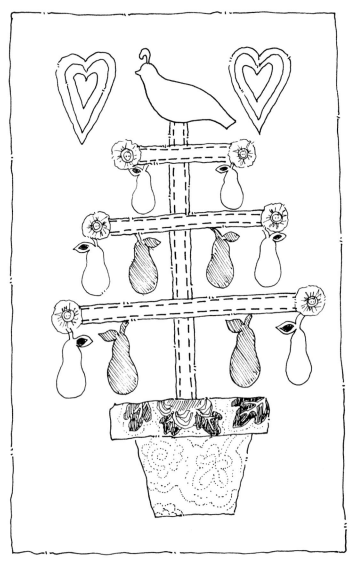

finishing

STEP 1 ✳ Assemble the quilt per the instructions on pages 12 and 13 and machine stipple (page 29) over entire quilt, excluding appliqués.

STEP 2 ✳ Sew the binding strips (2½" x 45") end to end. Bind per the instructions on pages 14 and 15.

Finished Size: 57" x 69"

Fox Creek Woods

When I was a little girl, one of our most cherished family traditions was to drive up in the mountains to find a Christmas tree. This always occurred on the day after Thanksgiving, and in Colorado, there is usually snow on the ground by then. Often, my mother stayed home (probably to have a little peace and quiet), while our father piled all of us into our old 1953 Chevrolet to go get the tree. We drove for what seemed forever (and was probably under 30 miles) up into the mountains behind Fox Creek. In those days, no one had four-wheel-drive vehicles, and worse than that, all the vehicles had rear-wheel drive. But our car had the durability of an army tank. It was almost inevitable that as we pulled off the gravel road we would end up getting stuck in mud. My father was always pretty calm (and competent), so we walked off to find the perfect tree, chopped it down, loaded it into the trunk, then went about the business of getting the car out of the mud. Usually, with a little shoveling, arranging some branches under the tires, and a little pushing, we got the car out and were on our way home, singing Christmas carols at the top of our lungs. During the few tense moments of getting the car out, I always hoped the angels would assist us, and I suppose they always did, for we always arrived home where our mother had her homemade cocoa waiting to warm us!

materials

⅔ yd. dark green print fabric for trees
⅓ yd. dark green floral print fabric for trees
¾ yd. tomato print fabric for trees
½ yd. tomato plaid print fabric for trees
1½ yd. dark taupe print fabric for angel block background
⅓ taupe mini print fabric for trees
1¼ yd. tea-dyed solid for border, legs, arms and faces
Fat quarter purple print fabric for block intersections
½ yd. cranberry floral fabric for binding
4½ yd. for backing
Scraps for clothing
Scraps of yarns and fibers for hair
65" x 77" piece of thin cotton batting
Embroidery floss: wheat, 3 skeins; brick red, 4 skeins; country red; pine green; medium taupe; black; light rose, I skein
12 red wooden buttons
Acrylic paint: rose
Small round stencil brush

cutting instructions

STEP 1 * Using the patterns from the pattern insert and various scraps, trace, stitch, trim seam allowance and complete 10 angels, following the Double Appliqué method on pages 8 and 9. The arms, legs and faces are made from the tea-dyed fabric.

STEP 2 * Using the purple print, cut out and prepare 12 squares (2½") for the block intersections, following the Double Appliqué method on pages 8 and 9.

STEP 3 * Using the pattern from the pattern insert, trace, and cut 20 triangles from the dark green print.

STEP 4 * Using the pattern from the pattern insert, trace, and cut 20 small trapezoids from the dark green print and 20 small trapezoids from the dark green floral print.

STEP 5 * Using the pattern from the pattern insert, trace, and cut 30 large trapezoids from the tomato print.

STEP 6 * Using the pattern from the pattern insert, trace, and cut 30 small trapezoids from the tomato print.

STEP 7 * Using the pattern from the pattern insert, trace, and cut 30 small trapezoids from the tomato plaid.

STEP 8 * From the taupe mini print, cut seven strips (1½" x 45"). Cut 20 strips to 13½" lengths for the tree block bases.

STEP 9 * From the taupe floral print, cut 10 squares (12¾") for the angel blocks.

tree block assembly

STEP 1 * The first row is assembled so there are two dark green triangles surrounded by three large tomato print upside-down trapezoids.

STEP 2 * The second row is assembled in a similar manner, with the floral green small trapezoids upright and the tomato plaid small trapezoids upside-down. The third row is assembled in the same manner as row two, using the dark green small trapezoids upright surrounded by the tomato print small trapezoids upside down.

STEP 3 * Sew the first and second rows together so the green fabrics are centered.

STEP 4 * Sew the third row to the second.

STEP 5 * Sew the taupe mini-print strips to the bottom of the trees.

STEP 6 * Trim the excess fabric from the sides and top to create 12¾" squares. Make 10 squares.

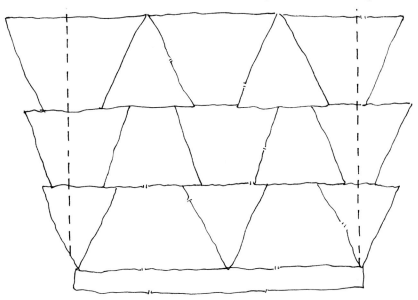

angel block assembly

STEP 1 * Layer and then stitch each angel to the center of a 12¾" dark taupe print block.

STEP 2 * Use a single thread for the embroidery. Refer to the stitch instructions on pages 19-25 for all embroidery. Embroider the angel faces. Stem stitch the nose using taupe floss, French knot the eyes using black floss, and straight stitch the lips with rose floss.

STEP 3 * Use scraps of yarn and fibers to fashion hair for each angel. Stitch to secure in place.

STEP 4 * Scraps of fabric are used to create bowties. Tear into ½" or ⅝" strips. Tie in center and trim ends.

STEP 5 * Referring to page 17, use the rose acrylic paint to dry brush the cheeks.

quilt top assembly

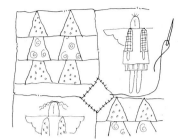

STEP 2 * Stitch a purple square appliqué to each inside intersection of blocks. The square is placed on the diagonal.

STEP 3 * Use pine green floss to attach a red wooden button to the center of each purple square.

STEP 4 * Sew the six border strips (5" x 45") end to end. Sew these to the sides, top and bottom edges of the quilt.

STEP 5 * Using the pattern from the pattern insert, trace pine branches and berries at each corner of the border. See page 10 for instructions.

STEP 6 * Using one thread for the pine branches and a full 6-ply strand for the berries, embroider the corner designs. Stem stitch the branches using medium taupe floss, straight stitch the needles with pine green floss and French knot the berries with country red floss.

STEP 1 * Assemble the blocks so there are four across and five down, alternating angels and trees.

finishing

STEP 1 * Sew the seven binding strips (2½" x 45") end to end.

STEP 2 * Assemble and bind the quilt per the instructions on pages 12-15.

STEP 3 * Using a full strand of wheat floss, stitch a running stitch along the inside of the angel blocks and brick red on the inside of the border. Refer to the photo and diagrams for placement.

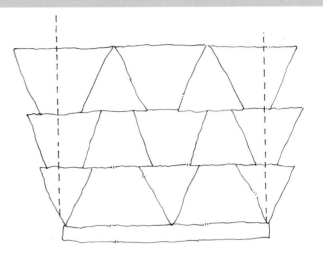